the **shotokan**
KARATE BIBLE

Acknowledgments

I would like to thank Nita Martin, without whom this book would never have happened. I would also like to thank the following people: Peter Terry and Denzil Fernandes at The Leys School for their help in arranging a venue for the photoshoot; Hiro Omori for supplying the Japanese script; all those who helped in the photoshoot: Nita Martin, Nick Day, Chris Day, Tom Davidson, Tom Auld, Ben Middleton, Jonathon Burnip, and Andrew Kuc.

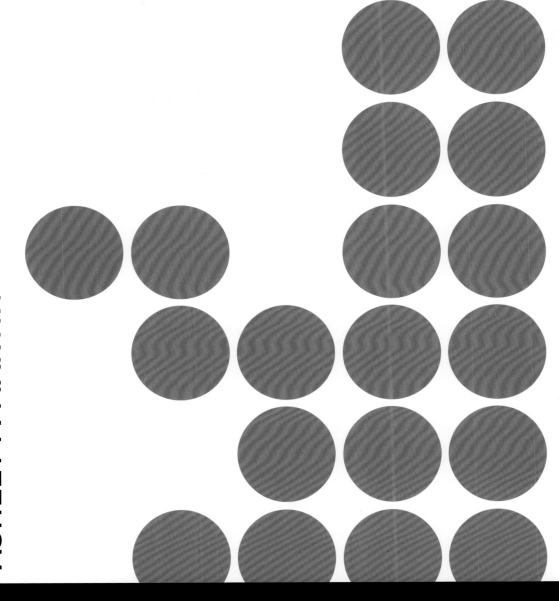

ASHLEY P. MARTIN

the **shotokan**
KARATE BIBLE
BEGINNER TO BLACK BELT

Bloomsbury USA
An imprint of Bloomsbury Publishing Plc

50 Bedford Square
London
WC1B 3DP
UK

1385 Broadway
New York
NY 10018
USA

www.bloomsbury.com

BLOOMSBURY and the Diana logo are trademarks of Bloomsbury Publishing Plc

First published 2007

British Library Cataloging-in-Publication Data
A catalogue record for this book is available from the British Library.

Library of Congress Cataloguing-in-Publication data has been applied for.

ISBN: PB: 978-1-63286-342-3
       ePub: 978-1-63286-343-0

2 4 6 8 10 9 7 5 3 1

Typeset in 9.5/13.75pt MetaPlusNormal by Margaret Brain
Printed and bound in China by C&C Offset Printing Co.,Ltd.

To find out more about our authors and books visit www.bloomsbury.com. Here you will find extracts,
author interviews, details of forthcoming events, and the option to sign up for our newsletters.

Contents

Karate is a Japanese martial art based on techniques developed in Okinawa and China that focuses on self-defense using punches, kicks, and blocks. Despite this emphasis, other techniques such as joint locks, throws, and leg sweeps are also included in the system. Karate is one of the few martial arts to contain such a wide range of techniques.

This book is aimed at the student of shotokan karate. There are many styles of karate, for example goju-ryu, wado-ryu, and shito-ryu, but ultimately each style of karate teaches the same principles, just with a different emphasis. A punch is still a punch; a kick is still a kick.

The Shotokan Karate Bible is intended to be a guide for the karate student, from beginner right through to expert, when you would be tested to receive the coveted black belt. Studying from a book is no substitute for a good teacher, but it can complement training with a qualified instructor.

What Does Karate Mean?

Karate, written in kanji

Written in kanji, Japanese pictographs, the word "karate" is composed of two characters. The first, pronounced kara, means "empty" and has Zen connotations. The second pictograph, pronounced te, means "hand" and so karate can be translated as "empty hand."

The kara symbol is thought to have its origins in the Buddhist sunyata, the Sanskrit term for the ancient metaphysical concept of emptiness or nothingness. Gichin Funakoshi, the father of modern karate, wrote:

As a mirror's polished surface reflects whatever stands before it and a quiet valley carries even small sounds, so must the student of Karate-Do render their mind empty of selfishness and wickedness in an effort to react appropriately toward anything they might encounter. This is the meaning of the kara or "empty" of Karate-Do.

Funakoshi is saying that you need to empty your mind in order to take the most appropriate action. He is implying that the appropriate action is the righteous and moral thing to do. However, many take it to mean the correct action to take in order to succeed in a fight. If you clutter your mind, you can't think clearly. Thus, an empty mind is needed to practice good karate.

This, however, is not the original meaning of karate. The original pictograph for kara was quite different. In Japanese, it was a homonym: that's to say, it was pronounced in the same way, but it had a different meaning. It meant Tang, which was a Chinese imperial dynasty at the zenith of Chinese civilization that had a huge cultural influence on its neighbors. Tang was synonymous with China, and the original karate pictographs meant

"Chinese hand." In Okinawa, the same two pictographs were pronounced "tode" and many in Okinawa referred to them simply as "te," meaning hand.

Original form of karate, written in kanji

This change from the old ideographs for karate to the new occurred at the beginning of the twentieth century. Japan was very nationalistic at this time, and, for many, the association of the old symbol with China was not acceptable. Some karate schools, particularly in Tokyo, began writing karate with hiragana, Japanese phonetic characters, as a way of avoiding the "inappropriate" kanji with its Chinese connotation. Others had started writing "empty hand" using the new symbol for kara. At a meeting of Okinawan karate masters in 1936, the new way of writing karate was officially accepted.

History of Karate

Much of the history of karate is shrouded in mystery. This is sometimes explained as being a consequence of the fact that, before the twentieth century, martial arts were often practiced in secret societies. But a more significant factor seems to be the impact of the "Typhoon of Steel," the invasion of Okinawa in 1945 by American forces that completely flattened the cities of Naha and Shuri, destroying any written records of karate's early development.

An examination of the available details suggests a fascinating origin for karate in Okinawa: a crack team of royal bodyguards, a kind of nineteenth-century secret service, working as bureaucrats and palace officials by

day and developing and practicing a deadly unarmed fighting style by night.

CHINESE WAY OF THE FIST

Many accounts of the origin of karate trace its roots back to ancient China with the introduction of martial exercises into the Shaolin temple by a Buddhist monk called Bodhidharma in the sixth century. He traveled from India to the Shaolin temple in China and found the resident monks to be in a feeble condition. Bodhidharma instructed the monks in the courtyard and began to teach them the art of Shih Pa Lohan Sho (the 18 hands of Lohan), so that the monks could attain spiritual enlightenment while preserving their physical health.

This story may be more myth than history, but the Shaolin temple was certainly one source of the class of Chinese martial arts known as ch'uan fa, the way of the fist. Chinese ch'uan fa was certainly a major influence on the martial art that we today call karate. But few of the Chinese traditions have been continued by karate practitioners and so, to find the real birthplace of karate, we need to look at a small island in the East China Sea called Okinawa.

KARATE: AN OKINAWAN MARTIAL ART

The Ryukyu Islands are located in the East China Sea

Okinawa is the largest of the Ryukyu Islands, an island chain that extends 620 miles from southern Japan to Taiwan. Today, Okinawa Island is the capital of the Japanese Okinawa Prefecture, but it was once an independent nation with a separate language and culture.

Martial arts probably existed in Okinawa as early as the Chinese Tang Dynasty (618–906 AD), but they would have been quite different from the karate that we see today. Okinawa entered into a tributary relationship with China in 1372, which meant that Okinawa was a province of China and would send regular taxes to the Chinese Emperor. This relationship accelerated Chinese influences on Okinawan culture. There was a permanent Chinese mission resident in the Okinawan Royal Palace, and many of the officials brought with them ch'uan fa secrets. At this stage, it would have been a distinctly Chinese martial art.

A common misconception is that karate was started in Okinawa by peasants. Learning a martial art like karate takes a great deal of time and effort. Peasants spent all their time during the day working, often doing back-breaking work. It would take an extraordinary person to then engage in something as physically demanding as karate in the evening. In fact, the karate masters were invariably of the keimochi (noble) class.

Three cities on Okinawa are important to the story of karate's development: Naha, a large port; Tomari, a smaller port; and the royal city of Shuri, the capital city of Okinawa. Each city had karate masters with their own kata and traditions.

The karate that developed at Naha, known as Naha-te, can be characterized as being a soft-style martial art, using more circular hand and foot movements that flow from one to another, giving it a graceful appearance.

Karate that follows the Shuri-te tradition is described as a hard-style martial art and tends to use big, strong, linear movements. In the 1500s, the King Sho Shin had a castle built in Shuri, to act as his palace and the bureaucratic center of his kingdom. It was here that the linear karate, which would become shotokan karate, developed.

The Tomari traditions were rather similar to the Shuri traditions, largely due to the fact that many of the Tomari masters were originally from Shuri, having retired from royal service.

THE STYLES OF KARATE		
Style of Karate	*Founder*	*In the tradition of*
Shotokan	Gichin Funakoshi	Shuri-te
Goju-ryu	Chogun Miyagi	Naha-te
Shito-ryu	Kenwa Mabuni	Shuri-te and Naha-te

Naha-te and Shuri-te have quite different histories and origins. Our interest is in the development of shotokan karate, and so our attention will focus on the events that unfolded in Shuri.

Two key events occurred that made Okinawa a unique breeding ground for a new martial art:

- In 1429, Okinawa was unified under the first Sho Dynasty. Prior to this, Okinawa had suffered from internal conflict between warring clans. To help maintain order, the second Sho King, Sho Shin, disarmed the bickering warlords by introducing a weapons ban. The nobility, the keimochi, were instead set to work as bureaucrats.

- In 1609, the Japanese Satsuma Clan of Kyushu invaded Okinawa. They probably found the weapons ban quite convenient and ordered that it be continued. Only now the ban was enforced by the Satsuma Samurai, who wielded katana, the deadly Japanese longsword.

By 1650, the Japanese were operating a policy of National Seclusion, Sakoku, which barred Westerners from trading in Japan (with an exception for limited trade with the Dutch). This policy was extended to Okinawa. Officially, Okinawa was still a province of China, and so, to keep control of Okinawa while avoiding war with China, the Shuri officials were ordered to deny any connection with Japan.

To compound this situation, European and American ships started appearing on the Okinawan shores in the nineteenth century carrying explorers, missionaries, and whalers. This conflicted with the Japanese isolationism and put the officials at Shuri in a difficult and dangerous position. They were instructed not to allow trade with the Westerners but were also not permitted to explain that the King of Okinawa was subordinate to the Japanese.

Matters came to a head in 1853 when Commodore Matthew Perry of the United States Navy paid a visit to Okinawa. His objective was to open trade between Japan and the United States. He decided that a show of strength in Okinawa was needed as a prelude to his negotiations in Japan itself. Perry demanded that he be allowed to see the King to discuss a trade agreement. As usual, the Okinawan officials politely declined. Perry then landed a force of 200 marines armed with Springfield rifle-muskets, two cannons, and two brass bands, and paraded up to Shuri castle. Perry himself traveled on a sedan chair carried by Chinese coolies. Perry and his entourage marched up to the gates of the royal palace and demanded entry. The Shuri officials allowed him to enter the main hall, where he found the Regent and a small group of his staff. The Okinawans expected Perry to declare himself governor of Okinawa, but Perry had only

planned to demonstrate his strength, and, having made his point, he returned to his ship. It was a tense incident nonetheless, and coming face to face with 200 marines must have had an impact on the staff at Shuri. And, as so many of the karate masters of that day were employed as high-ranking members of the royal household, it is very likely that they would have been there facing Perry and his men.

Clayton (2004) suggests that this encounter at Shuri Castle, combined perhaps with the many presumed incidents that remain undocumented, had a fundamental influence on the development of karate. He suggests that karate was designed to deal with a "target rich" environment, which is to say that it is meant to be effective even when outnumbered and surrounded by opponents. He concludes the following:

- Spending more than a few seconds fighting each opponent would not be good enough—they would have to be dispatched very rapidly.

- Ground fighting would be suicide.

- Defending against opponents armed with firearms or swords was necessary.

SATUNISHI "TODE" SAKUGAWA (1733–1815)

Sakugawa studied under an Okinawan master of tode called Takahara. He learned White Crane style ch'uan fa from Kong Su Kung, the Chinese military attaché to the Okinawan court. (The name of this Chinese dignitary is a matter of controversy: Kong Su Kung might not have been his name but instead his rank.)

The Okinawan reading of the ideographs of Kong Su Kung can be read Kushanku, and Sakugawa is often credited with having created the kata Kushanku, which would later form the basis of the shotokan kata Kanku Dai and Kanku Sho. In shotokan karate, Kanku Dai is the "master" kata. It appears to contain segments from all the core shotokan kata and may well have been the precursor of the Heian kata.

Sakugawa is sometimes credited with creating the dojo kun, the school code, but more commonly it is attributed instead to Gichin Funakoshi. The dojo kun is recited in many karate schools to this day. Its most literal translation reads:

Each seek perfection of character
Each protect the way of truth
Each foster the spirit of effort
Each respect others
Each guard against impetuous courage

Dojo Kun
hitotsu, jinkaku kansei ni tsutomeru koto
hitotsu, makoto no michi wo mamoru koto
hitotsu, doryoku no seishin wo yashinau koto
hitotsu, reigi wo omonzuru koto
hitotsu, kekki no yū wo imashimuru koto

Perhaps Sakugawa's greatest legacy was his most famous student, Sokon Matsumura.

SOKON "BUSHI" MATSUMURA (1797–1893)
The Bodyguard
If there was one man responsible for the transformation of Okinawa-te from what was essentially a Chinese art to the new art of karate, it was Sokon Matsumura.

Matsumura started training with Sakugawa at the age of 14. He was determined to become the greatest fighter in the land. He went on to become master of military affairs in the royal court, a highly important position as it would have meant that he was responsible for the safety of the King. After the capture of Okinawa by the Satsuma Clan, the King was required to spend half the year in Kyushu. Naturally, Matsumura traveled with the King, and it was during this time that Matsumura learned the sword fighting art of Jigen Ryu Kenjutsu.

Legend has it that Matsumura was given the title Bushi, meaning warrior, by the King Sho Ko after he fought a bull unarmed. The King had announced that, as entertainment, his great bodyguard, Matsumura, would battle a raging bull (some accounts say that the bull was a present from the Emperor of Japan). Everyone was invited to watch the great spectacle. Matsumura had to accept the challenge or lose face. On the appointed day, he turned up to face the bull. He stared into the bull's eyes, and it turned around and bolted. He had defeated the bull just by looking at it!

Matsumura had accomplished this apparent miracle by careful preparation. On discovering the impossible task he had been set, he went to visit the bull, taking with him a long pin. He looked into the eyes of the bull and poked it on the nose. He repeated this every day, up to the day of the challenge. He thus trained the bull to fear his gaze and so actually won through careful planning.

Over time, Matsumura served as chief bodyguard to a total of three Okinawan kings: King Sho Ko, King Sho Iku, and King Sho Tai. All three of these kings were deposed by their Japanese masters. The last, Sho Tai, was ousted at the beginning of the Meiji Restoration, when the Kingdom of Ryukyu became the Okinawa Prefecture. Sho Tai was abducted and taken to Japan, where he lived out his final days in exile. The aristocracy was abolished, and this would have put Matsumura and all the other Shuri officials out of work.

Matsumura would have been in service at the time that Perry made his historic visit to Shuri, and, given his position, it is quite likely that he would have been in that hall standing at the Regent's side facing 200 marines. This event may have influenced the direction of Matsumura's training and so have helped shape modern karate.

ANKO ITOSU (1830–1915)
The Big Kata Man
Itosu worked alongside Matsumura as secretary and translator to the King of Okinawa. But he was also, presumably, an apprentice bodyguard to the King under Matsumura. He trained and worked alongside Matsumura for 30 years.

Itosu was heavily built and had a reputation both for being very strong and for being able to withstand heavy blows. Funakoshi says that he had "the silhouette of a barrel" and that he could crush bamboo with his bare hands.

In 1901, Itosu introduced karate into the physical education system at an elementary school in Shuri. This was the same year that King Sho Tai died in exile, and it is possible that this was no coincidence. Once there was no chance that the King would return, perhaps Itosu felt released from any vows of secrecy he had taken while a royal bodyguard.

In 1908, he wrote a letter to the Prefecture Educational Department outlining the benefits that karate had to offer and encouraging the introduction of karate into all Okinawan schools. His suggestion was well received, and karate became part of the school curriculum in Okinawa. This made karate instruction available to the masses for the first time: the veil of secrecy over karate had been well and truly lifted.

Itosu's greatest legacy is his contribution to karate kata. He decided that some relatively easy kata were needed for teaching to middle school students. He invented the Pinan kata, which in the shotokan system are known as the Heian kata. These kata were possibly based on the Kanku kata, combined with moves from a long-forgotten kata called Chanan. Other kata that Itosu is reputed to have created are Naifanchi Nidan and Sandan, which later became known as Tekki Nidan and Sandan. An alternative theory is that the three Tekki kata were originally one long kata and that Itosu split them up. He also standardized the versions of Kanku Sho and Kanku Dai that are based on the kata Kushanku.

ANKO AZATO (1828–1906)
The Invisible Man of Karate

It seems that there are no surviving pictures of Azato and very little is written about him, which makes him a bit of a mystery man. Most of what we know comes from the writings of Gichin Funakoshi, who referred to Azato as the best martial artist he had ever met.

Like Itosu, Azato was one of Matsumura's students and held the position of foreign affairs advisor within the Shuri Royal Court. He was a member of the aristocracy.

He owned a castle and was a hereditary lord of the Azato village.

Funakoshi tells us that Azato challenged an armed sword master to a duel and defeated him with his bare hands by deflecting the sword with his arm before immobilizing his opponent. In another story, Azato and Itosu were confronted by thirty men, and so they fled into a nearby house. The men swarmed around the house, and the two decided that a fight was unavoidable. Azato leaped out of the window and started dispatching one hoodlum after another using a single blow each time, while Itosu dealt with the men around the other side of the house.

What is notable about this story is that it mentions that Azato and Itosu were using what is today called ikken hissatsu, one deadly strike, which represents the ability to defeat an opponent with a single devastating attack. This is one of the defining characteristics of modern shotokan karate.

Karate: A Japanese Martial Art

GICHIN "SHOTO" FUNAKOSHI (1868–1957)
The Father of Japanese Karate

Gichin Funakoshi was the school teacher from Shuri who is credited with bringing karate to Japan, thus earning himself the title of "Father of Modern Karate"(or sometimes "Father of Japanese Karate"). In fact, he wasn't alone in bringing karate to Japan. Many karate masters from Okinawa traveled to Japan to promote their art, including Kenwa Mabuni, founder of shito-ryu, which is a synthesis of Shuri-te and Naha-te, and Chojun Miyagi, founder of goju-ryu, which is based on the Naha-te traditions. But it was Funakoshi who did it first and perhaps did the best job of promoting it.

Funakoshi started studying karate under Anko Azato and later studied under Itosu. Funakoshi recalls that he spent ten years learning the three Naihanchi (Tekki) kata under Itosu. In 1913, as chairman of the Shobukai, the martial arts association of Okinawa, Funakoshi organized a group to travel around Okinawa performing public demonstrations of karate. It wasn't until 1916 that he was able to take karate to Japan, where he demonstrated at the Butokuden, the official center of Japanese martial arts. This event, and the demonstrations that followed, helped to bolster the popularity of the art. However, it was the visit of the Crown Prince of Japan, Hirohito, that really raised the profile of karate, and, in 1922, Funakoshi was invited by the Japanese Education Ministry to demonstrate karate at the first All Japan Athletic Exhibition in Tokyo. During his time in Japan, he stayed as a guest of Jigoro Kano, the creator of judo, and taught at the Kodokan, the judo school.

At the time that Funakoshi brought karate to Japan, the country was going through a very nationalistic phase, and anything that was not considered to be pure Japanese was regarded with suspicion or contempt. Karate, of course, was of Chinese and Okinawan origin. To overcome this perception, Funakoshi portrayed karate as following the Japanese budo (martial) tradition and made the following changes:

- The first ideograph in kara-te was changed from the old one that represented China to a new one meaning empty.

- Funakoshi adopted the uniforms and belt system of Kano's judo. Before this, there was no such thing as a karate black belt.

- Chinese culture was viewed with suspicion, but Zen Buddhism was not. Zen had a great deal of influence on Japanese culture and was considered an important part of Japanese budo. Karate's Shaolin origins were therefore emphasized alongside the adoption of the zen-like kara ideograph associating it with Zen Buddhism. This link was somewhat spurious because karate's development had been tied for so long to Okinawa, which had never really adopted Buddhism in the same way as Japan.

- Funakoshi attempted to change the kata names to Japanese words. For example, he renamed the Naihanchi kata to Tekki, but only a few of these new names persisted into the next generation of karate instructors, Funakoshi's own son included. Perhaps for them, the exotic Chinese or Okinawan names just had more flavor than the (from their point of view) mundane Japanese-sounding names.

Funakoshi invented the Taikyoku Kata and Ten No Kata, which were even simpler versions of Itosu's Pinan (Heian) kata, for teaching to elementary school students. However, according to one of Funakoshi's students, Shigeru Egami, these kata were in fact created by Funakoshi's son, Yoshitaka.

By 1935, Funakoshi had sufficient financial backing to build the first karate dojo, or training hall, in Japan. It became known as the Shotokan, after Funakoshi's pen name, shoto literally meaning "pine waves," and kan meaning "house."

SHOTOKAN KATA NAMES		
Okinawan/ Chinese Name	Funakoshi's New Japanese Name	Modern Shotokan Name
Pinan	Heian	Heian
Naihanchi	Tekki	Tekki
Seisan	Hangetsu	Hangetsu
Chinto	Gankaku	Gankaku
Niseishi	Nijushiho	Nijushiho
Wanshu	Empi	Empi
Rohai	Meikyo	Meikyo
Useishi	Hotaku	Gojushiho
Ji'in	Shokyo	Ji'in
Sochin	Hakko	Sochin
Chinte	Shoin	Chinte

YOSHITAKA "GIGO" FUNAKOSHI (1906–1945)

The Young Teacher

Gichin Funakoshi started the transformation of karate from an Okinawan to a Japanese art, but these changes were primarily ones of philosophy and nomenclature. However, Funakoshi's son, Yoshitaka (or Gigo, using a different reading of the ideographs for his name), really did transform the techniques of karate to produce what is essentially the shotokan karate that we practice today.

At a very young age, Yoshitaka was diagnosed as having tuberculosis, a terrible disease that, in 1913, was effectively a death sentence. Despite this, he engaged in his karate practice with great energy and spirit. He used very low, long stances and had a great love of sparring. He is said to have been responsible for the introduction of the side kicks, yoko kekomi and yoko keage, and the roundhouse kick, mawashi-geri, into the shotokan karate system.

The two Funakoshis shared the teaching at the Shotokan. The soft-spoken Gichin would teach his karate with high stances in the afternoon. The spirited and outspoken Yoshitaka, who was referred to by the students as waka sensei, young teacher, would teach his low stances, big punches, and high kicks in the evening. Yoshitaka sadly succumbed to a lung infection in 1945 and died. Despite this, it is clear that it is Yoshitaka's method that lives on in modern shotokan karate.

Following the Second World War, the occupying American forces placed a ban on martial arts in Japan because they were thought to have fostered regimentation and militarism. Karate managed to continue largely due to its emphasis on being a do, a way of life, which had spiritual goals and positive health applications rather than militaristic objectives.

As it turned out, the occupying forces weren't to be the end of karate but instead a great force in popularizing it. There was a great deal of interest in karate from servicemen stationed in Japan, and many of them trained with karate schools there and then took this strange new art with them back to their home countries.

HOW THE WEST WAS WON

Following the Second World War, there was growing interest in all things Oriental in the West, but karate still remained relatively unknown. In Ian Fleming's *Goldfinger*, which was first published in 1959, Goldfinger is talking to James Bond:

Have you ever heard of karate? No? Well that man is one of the three men in the world that have achieved the black belt in karate.

Fleming's view is that Bond, who is already introduced as being an expert in unarmed fighting, wouldn't have heard of karate. This tells us just how obscure karate must have been in 1959, which seems extraordinary today with every town having multiple karate clubs and terms such as "karate kick" or "karate chop" being part of everyday language.

The first public demonstrations of karate in the United States took place in Hawaii, where there was already a large population of Japanese and Okinawans. A number of masters of Okinawan karate visited Hawaii in the 1920s and 1930s, but the most notable was Chojun Miyagi, founder of the Goju-ryu style of karate, who remained in Hawaii from May 1934 until January 1935. His classes were marketed as "kempo karate." Kempo is the Japanese reading of the characters for the Chinese ch'uan fa, the way of the fist.

The kempo karate "brand' was later reused by the Hawaiian-born William Chow (1914–1987). Chow studied Koshu Ryu Kempo under James Mitose, and it is important to understand that this was very much a Chinese art, not to be confused with the uniquely Okinawan art that Gichin Funakoshi had taken to Japan and that would become shotokan karate. When Chojun Miyagi had referred to his art as kempo karate, it was probably a reflection of its mixed Chinese and Okinawan heritage. Chow, however, probably used the word karate simply because, at the time, it was a more familiar term in Hawaii than kempo. The result was that karate became associated with a much broader class of martial arts than just the fighting style of Okinawa.

Of the many students that William Chow promoted to the rank of black belt, the most influential was Ed Parker, who would become known as the "Father of American Karate." Parker was born in Hawaii and was introduced to kempo in the 1940s. After receiving his black belt grade in 1953, he moved to California, where he opened his first dojo in 1956. As a student of Chow, he initially called his art kempo karate, but in later years, and after further development, he renamed it American Kempo. Parker was a gifted businessman and was a major force in promoting karate throughout America and Europe by opening dojos, giving seminars, and organizing his International Karate Championship, which was notable for hosting the impromptu exhibition match between Bruce Lee and Chuck Norris in 1964. Parker also trained stunt men and celebrities, including Elvis Presley, who had a great interest in karate since he had been introduced to it during his time in the army.

THE KARATE CORPORATION

One organization that was active in this expansion was the Nihon Karate Kyokai, the Japan Karate Association (JKA), which was founded in 1948 with Funakoshi named as Chief Instructor. At that time, the JKA was based on the clubs studying Funakoshi's karate in the Tokyo area, and in fact almost all the senior JKA members were from the university clubs of Takushoku, Waseda, and Keio. Karate quickly spread under the JKA as it actively promoted karate worldwide by sending the graduates of its instructor training program all over the world.

One of these instructors was Hidetaka Nishiyama who, in 1953, was invited by the US Air Force on a sponsored tour of air bases in mainland United States to teach special courses for the personnel. Like so many of the original JKA instructors, Nishiyama had first trained in judo and kendo. He began his karate instruction under Gichin Funakoshi and in 1949 became captain of Takushoku University's karate team. After his move to America, he formed the All American Karate Federation (AAKF) and would later become executive director of the International Traditional Karate Federation.

Another JKA instructor who was sent to the United States by the JKA was Teruyuki Okazaki. While Nishiyama was based on the West Coast, in California, Okazaki was based on the East Coast, in Philadelphia. He created the East Coast Karate Association, which was initially affiliated with Nishiyama's AAKF but in 1965 broke away and formed the International Shotokan Karate Federation. In Europe, the JKA was represented by Hirokazu Kanazawa and Keinosuke Enoeda. Kanazawa was one of the first to graduate from the JKA instructor training program and was the All-Japan Karate Champion from 1957 until 1959. He became Chief Instructor of the Karate Union of Great Britain (KUGB) in 1966 before moving to Germany in 1968. Enoeda, who became known as "The Tiger," was a Takashoku graduate and winner of the All-Japan Karate Championship in 1963. He took over leading the KUGB on Kanazawa's departure.

SHOTOKAN SPLITS

In 1957, Gichin Funakoshi passed away. He did not name a successor, and his students split into two groups. One group called themselves shotokai (meaning Shoto's Group) and were led by Shigeru Egami. They were traditionalists who did not approve of the commercialization of karate or the growing popularity of competitive karate. The other group was the more radical JKA, led by Masatoshi Nakayama, who referred to their style as shotokan. The JKA promoted competition and organized the first Japanese karate championship in 1957.

It was in 1986 that the then head of the JKA, Masatoshi Nakayama, passed away, and leadership was passed to Nobuyuki Nakahara. However, his appointment was challenged by a number of JKA masters. Subsequent political infighting led to a major split resulting in two main factions: one led by Tetsuhiko Asai, who appointed Mikio Yahara as Chief Instructor, and the other headed by Nakahara, who named Motokuni Sugiura Chief Instructor. Following the split, legal disputes continued for many years over everything including who could legally use the JKA name and who had ownership of the headquarters building, the JKA Honbu. So for a period there was a peculiar situation in which two groups called themselves the JKA. In 1999, the Sugiura group won the exclusive right to the JKA name in Japan, and the Asai group renamed themselves Japan Karate Shotokai (JKS).

The political infighting is largely irrelevant to the many people practicing karate throughout the world. There are too many karate associations to count, but they do broadly practice the same karate techniques and follow the same customs that were taught by Gichin and Yoshitaka Funakoshi in Tokyo at the beginning of the twentieth century.

The typical karate class involves rows of white uniformed students moving up and down a hall punching, kicking, and shouting, with an instructor giving instructions in Japanese. This chapter explains many of the customs traditionally followed in karate classes and some of the terms used when talking about karate.

The Uniform

The karate uniform, which is called a dogi or more commonly just a gi, is traditionally made of white cotton. The karate gi is based on the judo gi but over the years has evolved from the heavyweight material of the judo gi into a lighter uniform. The karate gi also has ties on both sides of the jacket, which are not present on the judo gi. When tied, they help to keep the uniform together. The judo gi is held together solely by the belt.

Because of the karate uniform's lighter weight, it cannot take the same punishment as the judo gi. If someone grabs your jacket and tries to throw you, the karate gi may tear. One way to avoid this is to leave the ties untied, which will tend to result in the jacket just getting pulled out of the belt but not tearing.

Many karate schools will insist that students wear an ironed gi. The key is to look tidy!

The Karate Tripos: Kihon, Kata, and Kumite

Karate practice can be considered to consist of three components: kihon, kata, and kumite.

Kihon means "basic." When you practice kihon, you

The karate uniform is called a dogi

focus on repeating the basic techniques that form the foundation of all the other elements of karate. Often, kihon involves moving up and down the training hall performing a single technique or a short combination of techniques.

Kata means "form" or "pattern." In the context of karate, this means a sequence of prearranged techniques against imaginary opponents. Traditional karate styles are largely defined by their kata. There are two approaches to viewing kata. One is to view it as a performance art where the kata is performed purely for its own sake and where the aesthetics of the form are paramount. The other approach is to view the kata as a catalog of fighting moves that have some practical application for self-defense.

Kumite means "sparring" and is performed with a training partner. At the beginner level, this consists of basic five-step sparring (kihon gohon kumite) and basic one-step sparring (kihon ippon kumite). These are performed using formal positions and prearranged attacks and defenses. At the advanced level, this develops into free one-attack sparring (jiyu ippon kumite), where the positions are less formal but the attacks are still prearranged.

The most advanced level of kumite practice is free sparring, jiyu kumite, in which anything goes as long as it's within the realms of safety. This is also sometimes referred to as randori, which translates as "disordered engagement." A common and safe form of free sparring is practiced at slow speed but is continuous, and all techniques are allowed including grabs, elbow strikes, and throws. A more common form of free sparring, sometimes called shiai kumite, tournament sparring, is done with full speed techniques but with restrictive rules on what techniques can be used and with interruptions each time a point is scored.

Dojo Etiquette

Karate begins with a bow and ends with a bow

The karate training hall is called the dojo, which literally translated means "place of the way." Some karate schools use a dojo that is for the sole purpose of karate training, but most dojos are sports halls that are used only part time by a karate school. Whatever its physical nature, within the karate dojo you will be expected to follow certain rules of conduct.

GENERAL BEHAVIOR

Practicing karate should be fun, but it should nonetheless be remembered that some of the activities can be dangerous if done casually and with complacency. Therefore, always treat your teacher and your fellow students with respect:

- Keep toenails and fingernails short.
- Do not wear jewelery during training.
- Keep your training uniform clean and in good condition.

- Show respect to each other by not talking, swearing, or disrupting the lesson.

PARTNER WORK

- When training with a partner, the objective is mutual improvement of your karate, not to hurt each other.
- Never lose your temper.
- Always show control. You should never cause injury to your partner.

THE INSTRUCTOR

- Show your instructor respect. As a sign of respect, you should refer to your instructor as sensei, which means teacher.
- Pay attention to what your instructor tells you and be especially mindful of instructions regarding safety.
- If you are late for a session, wait for the instructor to indicate that you may join in.

BOWING

Bowing is very common in karate classes. In some schools, there is a bow every few minutes. In other schools, there are almost no bows. The most important times to bow are as follows:

- At the beginning and end of the class.
- At the beginning and end of a kata performance.
- Before you start sparring with a partner and then at the end when you are finished sparring.
- Whenever your instructor tells you to bow. This might be with the instruction rei, which means bow.

Several types of bow are used in Japanese culture. The most common bow in the karate class is the standing bow.

1 Start with your heels together. This is musubi-dachi (literally meaning "connected stance").

2 Keeping your hands at your sides and your back straight, gently bend from the waist.

3 Complete the bow by straightening up again.

1   **2**   **3**

Partly due to the influence of Bruce Lee in the film *Enter the Dragon*, there is a belief that you should keep your eyes on your partner while you bow. If you do not trust someone enough to take your eyes off them, you should not be bowing to them at all!

Training Tips

To make good progress, the karate student should train in the dojo with an experienced instructor at least two hours per week. For the beginner, three or four hours per week is optimal. Generally, more than eight hours per week of intense training can be counterproductive because it may result in injuries.

Before engaging in intense training, always warm up. Other training that can help you improve your karate is described below.

STRETCHING

Stretching defines your freedom of movement. Lack of suitable flexibility can mean working against your own muscles as they reach the limits of their normal range. Good flexibility is essential for correct stances and effective kicks and to minimize muscle strains and injuries. For best results, try to stretch for 20–30 minutes per day.

STRENGTHENING

Strong legs are especially important in karate because they are the driving force behind all techniques. High kicks require not only flexibility but also strong legs and stomach muscles.

FITNESS

Improve your cardiovascular fitness through aerobic activities like jogging or cycling.

KEEP A TRAINING DIARY

Use a training diary to keep a record of what you have learned. Keeping a note of important points will help you to remember them. Often the significance may not be obvious until later. When you do have a question about how best to do a technique, you can look back through your journal to see if you previously had the answer. You should also keep a note of any unanswered questions. Later you can look for an opportunity to find an answer. Often an instructor will ask "Any questions?" Rarely does anyone have a question, but they should! If you have your questions ready in advance, you can take this opportunity to learn.

Kiai: The Martial Shout

Karate classes contain a lot of shouting. The martial shout used in karate is called a kiai, which literally translated means "spirit unity." It is comparable with the "grunt" used by tennis players when hitting the ball. Monica Seles was renowned for her grunt. Many players complained about it putting them off or disguising the sound of her racket hitting the ball, but she felt that the grunting simply helped her to generate more power in her shots. In karate, the kiai is indeed also used to distract the opponent as well as to help focus power. You should use kiai for the following reasons:

- To boost your confidence by psyching yourself up before a fight.

- To intimidate or unsettle an opponent.

- To help with breathing. Holding your breath while attacking is a common mistake, and shouting a kiai on the technique ensures a smooth exhalation.

The karate kiai is a martial shout

When uttering a kiai, you shouldn't be saying a specific word. Don't yell out "Kiai!" This would be a bit like screaming "Shout!" Ideally, avoid consonants altogether: something like "Ai!" or "Eia!" is best.

There are a number of circumstances when it is appropriate to use a kiai, and some when it is positively required:

- Shotokan kata typically contain two kiai points. The kiai is considered a technique in itself, and omitting it is a mistake.

- Use kiai at the beginning of a fight to boost your confidence and intimidate your opponent.

- Use kiai during sparring when you score a technique.

- During gradings, it is important to show strong spirit. Use kiai on the last technique of a sequence.

- Use kiai whenever your instructor tells you to.

Kime: The Art of Focus

Kime literally means "decision." In karate, it means to focus all one's strength and energy into each technique. *Kime-waza* means a decisive technique, one that would finish a fight in a single blow. Good karate consists of only decisive techniques, and this includes not just punches and kicks but blocks also. Thus all karate techniques are explosive and are delivered with maximum intensity in the shortest time possible. The only exception to this is when a technique is meant to be delivered at slow speed. In this case, the moves should be performed under tension in a slow, controlled manner. But these moves are not without kime: the kime is merely spread throughout the technique.

Distancing

Upon completion of a karate technique, the body's motion is abruptly halted and the final position held. This is accomplished by instantaneously tensing all the muscles of the body, coupled with exhaling at the point of completion of the technique. The tension is only momentary, and you should immediately relax the muscles. It is important that this tension happens only at the end of the technique: tensing the muscles when they are not needed will only slow down techniques.

This tensing of the body is often incorrectly called kime, but in fact the kime occurs before this. The point of kime, of decision, is the point where you make contact with your target, not at the point of maximum extension.

Misunderstanding this results in techniques that might look and even feel strong but are actually ineffective. The correct distancing for decisive techniques should be practiced by using a punching bag. When aiming techniques at your training partner, you should not use this distancing precisely because you do not want to injure him. In this situation, you should focus the technique so that it comes to a halt just before it makes contact.

1

Too near to the target. The arm has not had enough time to acquire its full speed, resulting in a weaker punch.

2

Too far from the target. The arm has reached the end of its extension and has been slowed down by itself. This is the distancing you should use when training with a partner.

3

Correct distancing. Contact should be made with the arm at about 70 percent extension.

Kata Performance

SPEED

In the basic kata, all individual techniques are intended to be fast moves. Each technique should be performed with explosive speed, starting and stopping abruptly. In between each move, relax and prepare mentally and physically for the next explosive move. More advanced kata use slow, tense moves that contrast with these fast moves.

MOVES SHOULD BECOME NATURAL

The advanced practitioner can perform kata almost without thinking. Through the constant repetition of kata, reactions are built up over time so that when a particular technique is needed, it is instinctive. The moves in the kata encode techniques with practical self-defense applications. In real situations, there will not be enough time to think, only time to react. You should therefore practice kata every day. This may simply involve running through the kata in your mind, as this will still help make the kata instinctive.

CORRECT FORM

Maintain the correct positioning of the stance and hand techniques. You must learn to be observant of small details and be able to reproduce what your teacher does.

MENTAL FOCUS

When you practice your kata, you should picture imaginary opponents. This will help you think about the meaning of the moves. Appear alert and perform with strong spirit: each move should be executed with conviction and passion. Look in the direction that you attack, and when you kiai, do it with spirit.

Japanese Commands

In karate classes, it is common to give some instructions in Japanese, even though it may not be the first language of the instructor or the students. This will vary from one karate school to another. Some instructors do not use any Japanese, but most will use at least some. The table below is a guide to some common instructions given in Japanese.

COMMON JAPANESE KARATE TERMS		
Japanese	*Meaning*	*Comments*
Hajime	Begin	Used in tournaments to start the fight or in class to start a combination.
Rei	Bow	
Seiretsu	Line up	In most classes you will be expected to line up in grade order.
Naore	Relax (literally translated as "put back into place")	Return to ready stance and remain ready for the next instruction.
Sensei ni	Face the teacher	
Shomen ni	Face the front	
Mawatte	Turn around	Used in line work when the class runs out of space and it is time to go back the other way.
Yoi	Ready	Stand in ready stance and await the next instruction.
Yame	Stop	
Yasume	Rest	

In addition to these, the instructor may also use Japanese terms for the various techniques used in karate. These terms are introduced throughout this book, and a summary can be found in the glossary.

Meditation

Some karate schools, generally the more traditional ones, have a period of meditation at the beginning and the end of the class. Some will have meditation only at the beginning or at the end. Many schools will omit meditation altogether. The format of this meditation period varies, but typically it is as follows:

1 The class lines up.

2 The instructor (or often the senior grade) says "Seiza." Seiza literally translated means correct sitting and is a kneeling position with the feet tucked under the buttocks.

3 The instructor announces "Mokuso," which means to meditate. At this point, you should place your left hand in your right with the palms up. In many karate schools, you should close your eyes, while other schools expect you to lower your eyes, focusing on the ground just in front of you.

4 You should meditate by relaxing and clearing your mind. This continues, typically for between 10 and 60 seconds, until the instructor announces "Mokuso yame," which means "meditation finished."

Meditation is performed in the seiza position

The meditation period at the beginning of the lesson is useful to put you in the correct mindset to begin training, allowing you to clear your mind of needless clutter. The meditation should leave you calm, relaxed, and focused. The meditation at the end of a lesson allows you to reflect on what you have learned.

The Belt System

The color of the karate belt signifies the grade of the wearer. The belt colors for each grade vary from organization to organization, but they always start at white and end at black. The following system is used in this book:

SHOTOKAN BELT SYSTEM		
Grade	Japanese	Belt Color
Ungraded		White
9th Kyu	kukyu	Orange
8th Kyu	hachikyu	Red
7th Kyu	shichikyu	Yellow
6th Kyu	rokyu	Green
5th Kyu	gokyu	Purple
4th Kyu	yonkyu	Purple with one white stripe
3rd Kyu	sankyu	Brown
2nd Kyu	nikyu	Brown with one white stripe
1st Kyu	ikkyu	Brown with two white stripes
1st Dan	shodan	Black
2nd Dan	nidan	Black
3rd Dan	sandan	Black
4th Dan	yondan	Black
5th Dan	godan	Black
6th Dan	rokudan	Black
7th Dan	sichidan	Black
8th Dan	hachidan	Black
9th Dan	kudan	Black
10th Dan	judan	Black

An enduring myth about the belt colors is that the colors originate from the belt changing color with age. The story tells us that the founders of karate never washed their belts. All their belts started out white but, as they were used, they grew discolored with sweat, grass stains, and dirt, becoming first yellow then going from green to brown and then finally to black.

It is a seductive story but certainly untrue. Apart from the fact that the belts would have been disgusting and smelly, it just wouldn't work—the belts might go yellow and brown, but surely they would rot and fall apart before going black!

The karate ranks and belts were not always part of the karate system. It was not until 1924 that Funakoshi awarded the first shodan ranks given in karate to Tokuda, Otsuka, Akiba, Shimizu, Hirose, Gima, and Kasuya. The belt system was in fact taken from judo in the 1920s by Gichin Funakoshi. It was therefore actually invented by Jigoru Kano. Originally, judo only had two belt colors, white and black, but Kano introduced a belt above black belt to recognize high-ranking black belts. This was made up of alternating red and white panels and was awarded to 6th, 7th, and 8th degree grades. This innovation was made after Funakoshi had adopted the belt system and so it was not reflected in the karate belt tradition.

In most organizations, there are ten dan grades, from 1st degree black belt up to 10th degree black belt, which is usually held by the head of the organization. However, many organizations do not use this many grades in their system, nor is there an upper limit on the number of dan grades that a system might use. Some organizations, for example the shotokai associations, limit the black belt grades to a maximum of 5th dan.

The first few dan grades are awarded based on physical ability and usually require attending a grading examination in the same way as for previous grades. The higher dan grades are awarded based more on teaching experience, leadership ability, service to the organization, and tenure.

Grading Examinations

In order to progress from one karate rank to another and to get your next belt, you will need to take a grading examination (commonly just called "gradings"). Typically there should be a minimum of three months between each grading, but this will depend on how much training you put in during that period.

Do not consider rank as something to use to measure yourself against others. Everyone is different. You should compete against yourself and not the person standing next to you in line. Gradings are cumulative: you need to know everything from previous gradings. Rank is not about how good a fighter you are. You are not required to be able to "defeat" anyone to achieve your rank.

GRADING TIPS

- Do not hold back at the grading. Give it everything you've got.

- Even if you make a mistake, keep going. Do not highlight the mistake by showing an emotional response to it.

- Relax. Worrying won't help. A major rationale behind the grading is to see how you cope under stressful situations.

The grading examiner will use the following criteria to judge your performance:

The color of the karate belt signifies grade

KEY GRADING REQUIREMENTS

Correct form	Correct stance and hand positions.
Power and speed	Techniques should be explosive (using kime).
Attitude	Eyes should be focused ahead, not at the ground. Techniques should be confident and vigorous. Use a strong kiai on the last technique in a sequence when performing kihon.
Timing	Hands and feet should finish at the same time. When sparring, do not start blocking before the technique gets near you. On the other hand, don't leave it so late that you get hit.
Distancing	Execute techniques to the optimal distance. Don't overreach or try blocking too near to your own body. Be aware of your natural comfortable range (know how long your arm is). When sparring, make sure your attack reaches your partner but is focused so that they are not hurt.

CHAPTER **THREE** beginner to orange belt

Getting started is the most difficult part of karate training for most people. Karate classes often train all levels of students together, and for the beginner this can be quite daunting. However, you should see this as an opportunity to see skills farther down the line and to gauge what you may expect your ability level to be after various amounts of training.

As a beginner, the most difficult skills to learn will seem to be coordination between the arms and legs and general spatial awareness. These alone can deter beginners from continuing their training.

Beginners should not expect too much too quickly. It can take several hours of training to get comfortable with the coordination. Karate training consists of repetitive exercises that, through long-term dedication, teach the body new reflex actions.

For the first grading, all the blocking and punching techniques are also stepping techniques. One hand technique corresponds to one step. So, if you step forward with the left foot, you should be doing a block or punch with the left hand.

Syllabus Summary

White belt gradings follow the following format:

WHITE BELT GRADING SYLLABUS	
Basics	
Stepping punch	Oi-zuki
Rising block	Age-uke
Outside block	Soto-uke
Inside block	Uchi-uke
Front kick	Mae-geri
Kata	
Kihon Kata (Taikyoku Shodan)	
Kumite	
Five-step sparring	Gohon kumite

Basic Form

NATURAL STANCES

Shizen-tai

The natural stances are so called because they are all variations on how you would stand naturally. They require no tension in the legs and have the weight distributed evenly between the feet.

In the formal attention stance, heisoku-dachi (literally translated as "closed feet stance"), the feet are together with the heels and big toes just touching.

In the informal attention stance, musubi-dachi (literally translated as "connected stance"), the heels touch but the feet point out diagonally in a "V" shape.

In the parallel-feet stance, heiko-dachi, the feet are parallel and one shoulder-width apart.

Hachiji-dachi is the same as heiko-dachi but with the toes pointing out slightly. It roughly translates as "figure eight stance" named after the Japanese kanji for the number eight which resembles the foot position of this stance.

Shizen-tai literally means "natural body." If your karate instructor says "Shizen-tai," he wants you to stand in hachiji-dachi, with your arms straight and your hands making fists held just in front of you at hip height. This is also called ready stance, yoi-dachi.

Heisoku-dachi

Musubi-dachi

Heiko-dachi

Hachiji-dachi

A common mistake when standing in shizen-tai is to stand with the feet too far apart. Here is a method for moving into heiko-dachi with correctly placed feet.

1

Start in heisoku-dachi, heels and toes together.

2

Move your toes out into musubi-dachi. Your heels should still be together.

3

Pivoting on the front part of your feet, push your heels out so that your feet are parallel. You can make this a smoother motion by bending your knees and dropping your weight slightly as you do this.

4

Pivoting on your heels, push your toes out slightly.

FRONT STANCE
Zenkutsu-dachi

Front stance is used for lunging attacks. There should be no more than one hip-width between the axis of the front foot and the rear heel. The stance should be at least two hip-widths long, preferably longer. Make sure that the front leg is bent sufficiently with about 60 percent of your body weight over the front leg. You should not be able to see your toes because they should be obscured by your front knee.

Long, low stances are characteristic of shotokan karate. A deep front stance is difficult to maintain, but it helps with the development of both leg strength and flexibility. It offers good balance and stability, but this is traded off against speed and mobility. At a higher level, you will learn to mitigate these drawbacks by using the front stance as a transitional position, holding it for only an instant before moving on to a higher, more dynamic stance. You should use as low and long a stance as you can when practicing the basic techniques in kihon, kata and kumite.

Front stance, zenkutsu-dachi

There are two hip positions that can be used when in front stance:

- The full front-facing hips position is achieved by pushing the hip forward with the back leg. In this position, your back knee must be straight.

- The half front-facing hips position involves pulling one hip back so that the chest faces 45 degrees to the side. In this position, your back knee will be slightly bent.

When moving in front stance, consider the following points:

- Move in a sliding motion while stepping with your feet touching the ground throughout, even if it is only a light pressure. Keep the heel down on your front foot.

- Do not allow your hips to bob up and down. Your hips should be driven forward in a straight line parallel with the floor.

- Keep your back and neck upright but in a natural posture, which is to say that your back should not be as straight as a board. Leaning very slightly forward is natural and preferable as a fighting posture. Leaning backward is a big mistake.

- Keep your knees pointing in the same direction as your feet. To do otherwise puts unnecessary stress on the ankles and could result in an injury.

- In front stance, your front foot should point forward. When stepping forward, this foot will twist out to the side as you finish the step, but make sure that this happens as late into the step as possible. A common error is to allow this to happen as the first action before stepping.

1

Start in front stance with your left leg in front.

2

Slide your right foot up to your left. Ensure that you keep your knees bent so that your hip height remains the same.

3

Continue moving your right foot so that you step forward, finishing in a long stance.

MAKING A FIST

Before you can punch or block, you need to make a fist. It is important to get this right or you could end up hurting your hands on impact.

It is important to keep the fist tight on impact because this offers protection to the fingers. Almost all karate techniques demand that you keep the wrist straight. This is especially important when punching.

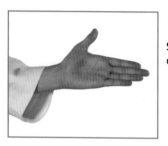

1

Start with your hands open.

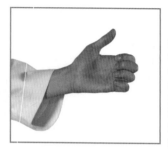

2

Starting with your fourth finger and finishing with your index finger, close the middle and top finger joints so that your fingertips touch the top of your palm at the base of your fingers.

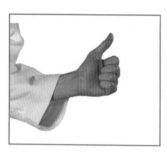

3

Continue to fold your fingers in tightly.

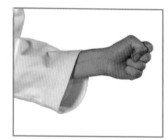

4

Fold your thumb in so that it touches the second (middle) phalanx of the index and second finger.

DOWNWARD BLOCK

Gedan Barai

Gedan barai (literal translation "lower-level sweep") is a downward block that can be used to defend against low-level attacks, deflecting them to the side. It is one of the most versatile moves in karate and can be used not just for deflecting incoming punches and kicks but also as an attack itself. It is usual in a karate class for gedan barai to be used every time you step forward ready to practice basic form. Your instructor will say something like, "step forward, gedan barai." This technique is also often used on turns when you are standing in front stance. The instructor will say "mawatte," which means "turn around."

In gedan barai, the opposite hip is pulled away from the block so that your hips and chest face to the side. This contrasts with the action used with the stepping punch, which is described in the next section. Ensure that you are still looking forward and that your front foot and knee point forward.

The opposite hand is pulled back to the hip so that it is on, or just above, the belt. This is known as hikite, meaning "pulling hand." This pulling action should be as strong as the blocking technique. Almost every time you do a technique in karate, you will have to use hikite, and a common mistake is to have a weak hikite or to leave it out altogether.

1 Start in ready stance.

Side view.

2 Prepare to block with your left arm.

Side view.

3 Block to the lower level by sweeping your left arm down across your body.

Side view.

STEPPING PUNCH
Oi-zuki

The stepping punch (or "chasing punch," which is the literal translation of oi-zuki) is a lunging attack used to cover a big distance. Power is generated mainly from the step, and so body weight must be put behind the punch. The punching hand should move in a straight line from the hip to the target and should be angled in slightly so that it hits in line with the center of the body. On completion of the technique, ensure that your hips and chest are squarely pointing forward and that the rear leg is straight.

1 Start in front stance, zenkutsu-dachi.

Side view.

2 Slide your right foot forward. Start to punch and withdraw the other hand.

Side view.

3 Step forward into zenkutsu-dachi and finish the punch at the same time. Rotate your fi t at the end of the punching action.

Side view.

Here are some training tips to help you punch correctly:

- Keep your elbows close to your body and behind the punch.
- Punch straight, with your fist t aveling in a straight line from your hip to the target.
- The fist of our punching hand should stay palm-up throughout the punch, then rotate at the end.
- Strongly pull the opposite hand (hikite) in the same way as with the downward block.
- Relax unnecessary muscles. Do not hunch the shoulders.

COMMON MISTAKES

Elbow comes out to the side

Lifting your elbow out to the side will turn the technique into more of a hook punch. This kind of punch swings in from the side and is very powerful, but this is not the type of punch you should be aiming for. Keeping the elbow close to the body will produce a straight punch that is much harder to defend against.

Incorrect   *Correct*

Fist drops below elbow

In this case, the elbow initially moves forward faster than the fist. This causes the fist to flick up at the end. Instead, keep your elbow behind your fist, driving it forward in a straight line.

Incorrect   *Correct*

Hand not retracted

Incorrect   *Correct*

Bad posture

Tensing your shoulder muscles may make you feel more powerful, but in fact it can just slow you down. Try to relax your upper body more while you throw the punch, generating the power by using your hips more than your shoulders.

Incorrect   *Correct*

INSIDE BLOCK

Uchi-uke

This block works by swinging your forearm across your body. It is most commonly performed as a defense against stomach level attacks but is equally effective against head level attacks. It can be used against straight attacks such as a stepping punch, deflecting the attack before it hits. However, inside blocks are most effective when stopping a circular attack such as a roundhouse kick or a hook punch.

The fist starts palm-side down in the preparation. It then rotates so that it is facing toward you at the end of the block. The blocking hand should move on the outside of the retracting hand. As you block, pull back the opposite hip and hand so that your chest faces to the side and your retracting hand finishes on your hip. Throughout the move, your blocking arm should be bent 90 degrees, and at completion your fist should be in line with our shoulder.

1

Start in front stance, zenkutsu-dachi.

2

Slide your left foot forward and prepare to block with your left arm by bringing your left fi t under your right armpit while reaching forward with your other arm.

Side view.

3

Step through with your left leg into front stance, zenkutsu-dachi, and block with your left arm. Note that the block must pass through and finish slight y to the left of your center-line.

OUTSIDE BLOCK

Soto-uke

This block sweeps from head level down across the body and can be used to defend against stomach level attacks, deflecting them to the side. The fist starts palm-side facing away from you in the preparation and rotates so that it is facing toward you at the end of the block. As you block, pull back the opposite hip and hand so that your chest faces to the side and your retracting hand finishes on your hip. Throughout the move, your blocking arm should be bent 90 degrees, and at completion your fist should be in line with your shoulder. This is similar to the inside block finish position.

1

Start in front stance, zenkutsu-dachi.

2

Slide your right leg forward and prepare to block with your right arm by lifting it behind you while reaching forward with your other arm.

3

Step through with your right leg into front stance, zenkutsu-dachi, and block with your right arm. Note that the block must pass through and finish slight y to the left of your center-line.

Side view.

RISING BLOCK
Age-uke

The rising block can be used to defend against head level attacks, deflecting them up over your head. Your blocking fist should move up the center-line of your body, as if doing an upper-cut. Your blocking hand should move on the outside of your retracting arm and rotate at the end of the block so that your palm is facing away from your head. As you block, pull back your opposite hip and hand so that your chest faces to the side and your retracting hand finishes on your hip.

1

Start in front stance, zenkutsu-dachi.

2

Slide your right foot forward and prepare to block by reaching forward with your left arm.

3

Step through with your right leg into front stance, zenkutsu-dachi, and block with your right arm.

Side view.

FRONT KICK

Mae-geri

Of all the kicking attacks, front kick is probably the fastest. It involves almost no upper body movement and so can almost seem to come from nowhere in a fight. It uses the ball of the foot as the striking area, which means that at the point of impact, you should point your foot but pull back your toes, as if you are standing on tip-toe. The front kick should be delivered as a snap kick, which means that once it hits its target it should be pulled back, like a tennis ball bouncing off a wall.

Try to lift the knee of the kicking leg as high as possible in preparation for the kick, but ensure that your body does not rise up. This can be achieved by aiming to drop your body weight while raising your knee.

1

Start in front stance, zenkutsu-dachi, with your arms out to the sides.

2

Raise your knee.

3

Kick. Strike with the ball of your foot.

4

Snap back before stepping forward.

COMMON MISTAKES

Poor knee lift

The higher you want to kick, the higher you will need to lift your knee. If you fail to lift your knee high enough prior to extending your leg, then your foot will swing up toward the target rather than shooting in a straight line.

Failing to retract foot

A common mistake is to allow the foot to fall directly to the floor after extending the leg. If you do this, it makes it easier for an opponent to catch your leg after you kick. Instead you should make sure that you snap your foot back before stepping down.

1

Throwing front kick, mae-geri, without snapping back allows an opponent to catch the leg.

2

With the leg trapped, it is easy to unbalance and take down an opponent.

REVERSE PUNCH

Gyaku-zuki

The reverse punch is the most commonly used counterattack. It is very popular in sports karate, and most scoring techniques in karate tournaments are with the reverse punch. The hips are thrown toward the target just ahead of the punch. Be careful not to overreach by bending your back. Keep upright throughout the technique, doing the work with your legs and hips. Remember to follow the same punching form as for stepping punch.

1

Start in front stance, zenkutsu-dachi.

Side view.

2

Punch with your right hand by throwing your right hip and chest forward. Try to push your shoulder as far forward as possible. Ideally you should aim for the shoulder of the punching hand to be farther forward than the opposite shoulder. However, ensure that you keep a good posture with your front knee bent and your body upright. Also, for maximum power delivery, it is important that this motion is achieved by pushing the punching side forward, not by pulling the opposite side back. Any backward motion can be considered as being subtracted from the net power of the technique.

41

Kihon Kata

Gichin Funakoshi created three Taikyoku kata: Taikyoku Shodan, Taikyoku Nidan, and Taikyoku Sandan. In general, the latter two kata are not taught by shotokan schools but are typically practiced in shotokai schools.

The first kata you will learn is Taikyoku Shodan. It acts as an introduction to kata before starting on the more sophisticated Heian kata. This kata is almost always called Kihon Kata (meaning basic kata) by shotokan schools.

Karate kata contain within them highly effective self-defense moves. In Chapter 11, there is an explanation of how kata can be used in realistic combat situations.

TRAINING TIP

In Kihon Kata, there are only two hand movements: downward blocks and punches. Ensure that these two moves are distinct. A downward block follows a curved path and finishes at low level. A punch follows a straight path and, in the kata, finishes at stomach level (ideally at the height of your solar plexus, but at the very least ensure that it is lower than your shoulder and higher than your hip).

STARTING AND FINISHING THE KATA

Kihon Kata (and all the Heian kata) start and finish in the same manner. The procedure for starting and finishing is as much a part of a complete kata performance as any of the actual techniques of the kata.

When finishing, hold the last position until told to relax. Then bow to finish.

1

Start in ready stance, yoi-dachi.

2

Put your feet together in musubi-dachi. Bow and announce your kata in a loud and confident manner.

3

Step into ready stance.

KATA SEQUENCE

Bow. Announce kata "Kihon" and step into ready stance, yoi-dachi.

1

Step to the left and downward block, gedan barai, to the left.

2

Stepping punch with your right hand.

3a

Move your right foot as if stepping backward and start turning clockwise. At the same time, prepare for downward block, gedan barai, by extending your left arm and bringing your right fist alongside your left ear.

3b

Complete the turn so that you face the opposite way, and execute right-side downward block.

4

Stepping punch with your left hand.

5

Step to the left and downward block, gedan barai, with your left arm.

6

Step forward and punch with your right hand.

7

Step forward and punch with your left hand.

8

Step forward and punch with your right hand. Kiai.

9a

Move your left foot around behind you and start turning counterclockwise. At the same time, prepare for downward block, gedan barai by extending your right arm and bringing your left fi t alongside your right ear.

Side view.

9b

Continue turning so that you go through 270 degrees. Slide your left foot out into front stance, zenkutsu-dachi, and execute left-side downward block, gedan barai.

10

Step forward and punch with your right hand.

11

Move your right foot as if stepping backward and then pivot, turning 180 degrees, and execute right-side downward block, gedan barai.

12

Step forward and punch with your left hand.

13

Step to the left and downward block, gedan barai, with your left hand.

14

Step forward and punch with your right hand.

15

Step forward and punch with your left hand.

16

Step forward and punch with your right hand. Kiai.

17

Move your left foot around behind your right then off to the side so that you turn 270 degrees. Step into front stance, zenkutsu-dachi, and execute left-side downward block, gedan barai.

18

Step forward and punch with your right hand.

19

Move your right foot as if stepping backward and then pivot, turning 180 degrees, and execute right-side downward block, gedan barai.

20

Step forward and punch with your left hand.

Move your left foot back into ready position and finish with a bow.

Sparring Forms

Kumite

Sparring (kumite) is an exercise performed between two karate practitioners where the objective is to work together to improve technique, targeting, distancing, and timing. The objective is not to injure your partner, nor is it to "win" a fight.

There are many variants of kumite. At beginner level, it takes the form of five-step sparring, gohon kumite, where all the attacks, blocks, and counters are prearranged. The example below shows one-step sparring, ippon kumite. In five-step sparring, step 2 is repeated an additional four times and a kiai is added to the last punch only.

BOWING

Before you start sparring, bow to your partner. This shows respect and is a signal to say that you are now ready. When you have finished the sparring sequence, bow again. This again shows respect but also is a signal that you are finished and do not expect any more attacks!

HEAD LEVEL (JODAN) ATTACK

1

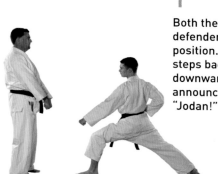

Both the attacker and the defender start in ready position. The attacker steps back with a downward block and announces the attack: "Jodan!"

2

The attacker steps forward and punches, targeting the head. The defender steps back and blocks with a rising block. This is repeated four more times during five-step sparring (but only kiai on the fifth attack).

3

The defender counter-attacks using reverse punch with kiai. The punch should be focused so that it just makes contact. It should not hurt your opponent but must not fall short. The attacker withdraws and, as he does so, the defender steps up, both finishing in ready stance, yoi-dachi.

STOMACH LEVEL (CHUDAN) ATTACK

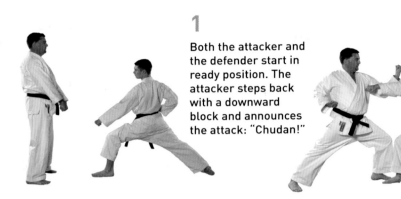

1

Both the attacker and the defender start in ready position. The attacker steps back with a downward block and announces the attack: "Chudan!"

2

The attacker steps forward and punches, targeting the body. The defender steps back and blocks with an outside block. This is repeated four more times in five-step sparring (but only using kiai on the fifth attack).

3

The defender counterattacks using a reverse punch with kiai. The punch should be focused so that it just makes contact. It should not hurt your opponent but must not fall short. The attacker withdraws, and, as he does so, the defender steps up, both finishing in ready stance, yoi-dachi.

IMPORTANCE OF FIVE-STEP SPARRING

Although five-step sparring seems simple, it has benefits for all levels. It helps develop a committed attitude to attacking and defending and helps with targeting and distancing skills.

Because there are five steps, any mistakes in the first step will be amplified in the following ones, something that will not happen in one-step sparring. If the defender is not stepping back far enough on each step, then by the fourth and fifth step they will find the attacker right on top of them and so will find it increasingly difficult to block effectively.

Ensure that you still use correct form to execute your techniques. This means using full preparations for the blocks, pulling back the reverse hand on punches, and using correct stances.

TARGETING

Ensure that your attacks are on target. If you don't, there will be no reason for your training partner to block. If you and your sparring partner tend to punch off target, then your blocking techniques will not have an opportunity to develop. When doing gohon kumite, your target areas should be those that are safest for your sparring partner. For jodan attacks, target the chin. For chudan attacks, target the stomach.

DISTANCING

You must ensure that you make the correct distance when punching. This is particularly important when counter-attacking. With correct distancing, you should make contact with your target, but, in order that you do not hurt your sparring partner, you should focus the attack on the target's surface.

If you find that you are too far away from your partner after you have blocked, you need to make more distance when counterattacking. Do this by pushing in your hip and bending your front leg. If this is insufficient, you will have to shuffle in as you punch.

COMMON MISTAKES

Overreaching

Don't try to extend your range by leaning forward. This will unbalance you so that the next step will be harder. It will also move your head nearer to your opponent, which in general is a bad idea while sparring. If you need to make more distance, do it using your legs, either by making a longer and deeper stance or by shuffling your feet nearer.

Incorrect form: attacker leaning into the attack

Leaning Forward When Blocking

Although this may feel like you're moving your stomach and groin out of range, you're actually moving your chest and face into range of the attack. In fi e-step sparring, you will find it harder to escape the next attack if you lean forward on the block. If the attacker's punch is far away, do not feel that you have to lean forward so that your block can reach. If the punch cannot reach you, don't worry about it. You do not need to block an attack that cannot hit you.

Incorrect form: defender leaning forward

Maintaining Front Stance

Make sure that you use correct stances. A common mistake is failing to bend the front leg. This will make it harder to make the correct distance to your target when you punch.

Incorrect form: attacker not bending the front leg

Attitude and Kiai

Do not underestimate the importance of strong attitude. Without strong attitude, your attacks will not be effective. Use a strong kiai to demonstrate good spirit and strengthen your resolve.

CHAPTER **FOUR** orange to red belt

kicks are not mastered until a much higher level. The orange belt level also introduces the knife-hand block, which is a key technique in shotokan karate and one which is often pivotal in kata performances.

Syllabus Summary

Orange belt gradings follow the following format:

ORANGE BELT GRADING SYLLABUS	
Basics	
Stepping punch	Oi-zuki
Rising block	Age-uke
Outside block	Soto-uke
Inside block	Uchi-uke
Knife-hand block	Shuto-uke
Front kick	Mae-geri
Side thrusting kick	Yoko kekomi
Side rising kick	Yoko keage
Kata	
Heian Shodan	
Kumite	
Five-step sparring	Gohon kumite

Basic Form

SIDE STANCE
Kiba-dachi

This stance is also called horse stance, rider stance, or straddle stance. The feet are placed about two shoulder-widths apart, with the feet parallel and facing forward. The weight must be evenly spread between the feet. Bend the knees and maintain an outward tension, pulling the knees outward. Kiba-dachi is good for developing both leg flexibility and strength and is also useful for close-range attacking and throwing. As with the front stance, keep your back and neck straight.

Side stance, kiba-dachi

BACK STANCE

Kokutsu-dachi

In this stance, the feet are placed two shoulder-widths apart, with the feet perpendicular to each other. The front foot should be facing forward and the back foot facing to the side. Most of the weight (about 70 percent) should be on the back foot. Bend the back leg, lowering the stance to the same height as in front stance. The front leg should be slightly bent, and the back should be straight and upright.

How to step forward when in back stance:

1

Start in back stance.

Side view.

2

Bring your knees together. Try to keep your hips at the same height.

3

Slide your right foot forward, keeping all the weight on the left foot.

4

Step forward into back stance by abruptly rotating your hips and pushing your right foot forward.

KNIFE-HAND BLOCK
Shuto-uke

This technique uses the outside fleshy part of the hand to block. It can also be used as a striking technique at close range against the neck. Unlike the other techniques, the retracting hand remains open and pulls back to protect the solar plexus, which is the soft spot along the center-line of the body just below the ribs. Although this technique is always called a block it can also be used as a strike.

1

Start in ready stance.

2

Drop your weight and start to slide your left foot forward. Prepare to block with your left arm by bringing it up to your shoulder with the palm facing toward your ear. Reach forward with your other hand, palm down.

3

Execute shuto-uke and step into back stance. The tips of your fingers should be at shoulder height and your arm should be bent at 90 degrees.

TRAINING TIPS

- Pull the elbow of your blocking hand in close to your center-line.
- Try to time the blocking action to coincide with the twisting of your hips as you settle into back stance.
- Keep your hands tense with your fingers together.

HAMMER FIST STRIKE

Tetsui-uchi

This strike is done with the fleshy underside of the fist. This version of the strike, sometimes called vertical hammer fist strike, swings down from over the head and can be used to attack the collarbone or the nose.

1 Start in front stance with gedan barai.

2 Pull back your leading hand. Do this by sliding your front foot back so that you use your whole body to drive the movement.

3 Swing your fist up over your head.

4 Slide your left foot forward again as you shift body weight back. Strike with the base of your fist at collarbone height.

TRAINING TIPS

- Make your arm and foot movements big, but don't pull your body weight back too far as it will slow down your subsequent forward motion.

- Finish with the elbow at 90 degrees.

SIDE RISING KICK
Yoko Keage

This kick is also known as side snap kick because, after the kick, the foot is pulled back in a whipping action. The direction of the kick is upward and can be targeted at the chin or armpit. The striking surface is the edge of the foot, not the toes, sole, or heel.

1

Start in side stance, kiba-dachi.

2

Step forward with your right foot crossing in front of your left. Keep your knees bent so that your hips remain at the same height throughout.

3

Lift your left knee so that it is pointing to the side with your left foot resting on your right knee.

4

Kick to the side. Use your hip to throw the kick. Rotate your supporting foot on the ball of the foot.

5

Snap back. This should be the reverse of the motion of step 4, pulling with your hip and rotating on the supporting foot. Your foot should return along the same path that it went out on.

6

Step down into side stance, kiba-dachi.

SIDE THRUSTING KICK

Yoko Kekomi

Ensure that the knee lift before the kick is high. Try to make your kicking foot go in a straight line to the target from this preparation position. Do not allow your kicking foot to drop down below the level you are kicking to. At the point of maximum extension, lock the kick in position, because this is a thrust kick. The striking area is the heel of the foot, with the foot pointing diagonally downward. Make sure that you bring the leg back to the recoil position (as shown in step 5) before stepping down: do not let the leg just drop to the floor after kicking.

1

Start in side stance, kiba-dachi.

2

Step forward with your right foot crossing in front of your left. Keep your knees bent so that your hips remain at the same height throughout.

3

Lift your left knee so that it is pointing to the front.

4

Kick to the side. Do this by rotating on the ball of your supporting foot and aiming the base of your foot at the target before extending your leg so that the kick follows a straight line. Hold your leg extended briefly, locking your muscles. Ensure that the supporting leg is bent. Feel like you are pushing your whole body weight into the target.

5

Pull the kicking leg back into the same position as in step 3. Your foot should return along the same path that it went out on.

6

Step down into side stance.

Heian Shodan

This is the first in the Heian series of kata. Heian simply translated means "peace." The Heian kata were created by Master Itosu at the beginning of the twentieth century. They were originally called the Pinan kata in Okinawa and were renamed in Japanese as part of the "Japanification" of karate by Gichin Funakoshi. He also re-ordered the kata: the shotokan kata we today call Heian Shodan was originally the second in the Heian series of kata, but Funakoshi presumably realized that the kata that was originally first in the series was much harder. Other styles of karate, such as wado-ryu, call this kata by the original name of Pinan Nidan.

KATA SEQUENCE

Bow. Announce kata "Heian Shodan" and step into ready stance, yoi-dachi.

1

Step to the left with downward block, gedan barai with your left hand.

2

Stepping punch with your right hand.

3

Slide your right leg straight back, then turn 180 degrees, and execute right-side downward block.

4

Execute hammer fist strike on the spot with your right hand.

5

Stepping punch with your left hand.

6

Step to the left with a downward block, gedan barai using your left hand.

7

Step forward and execute right rising block, age-uke.

8

Step forward and execute left rising block, age-uke.

9

Step forward and execute right rising block, age-uke. Kiai.

10

Move your left foot round behind your right, then off to the side so that you turn 270 degrees and execute left-side downward block.

11

Step forward and punch with your right hand.

12

Slide your right leg straight back, then turn 180 degrees, and execute right-side downward block.

13

Step forward and punch with your left hand.

59

14

Step to the left and perform downward block, gedan barai with your left hand.

15

Step forward and punch with your right hand.

16

Step forward and punch with your left hand.

17

Step forward and punch with your right hand. Kiai.

18

Move your left foot around behind your right then off to the side so that you turn 270 degrees and execute left-side knife-hand block.

19

Step forward at 45 degrees with a right-side knife-hand block.

20

Pivot on your left foot, turning 135 degrees, and execute right-side knife-hand block.

21

Step forward at 45 degrees with a left-side knife-hand block.

Finish by moving your left foot back into ready stance and bowing.

CHAPTER **FIVE** red to yellow belt

The red belt syllabus introduces the concept of attacking and defending with combinations of techniques, where one technique follows another. This can be a challenge of coordination at first, with students sometimes finding it hard to decide which hand to use next, but any difficulty is ultimately overcome by repetition of the combinations.

Syllabus Summary

Red belt gradings follow the following format:

RED BELT GRADING SYLLABUS	
Basics	
Triple punch	Sanbon tsuki
Rising block, reverse punch	Age-uke, gyaku-zuki
Outside block, reverse punch	Soto-uke, gyaku-zuki
Inside block, reverse punch	Uchi-uke, gyaku-zuki
Knife-hand block	Shuto-uke
Front kick	Mae-geri
Side thrusting kick	Yoko kekomi
Side rising kick	Yoko keage
Kata	
Heian Nidan	
Kumite	
Five-step sparring	Gohon kumite

Basic Form

TRIPLE PUNCH
Sanbon tsuki

This combination consists of a stepping punch followed immediately by two punches on the spot. Ensure that all the punches are lined up with the center of your body. Each time you punch, make sure you retract the other hand back to the hip.

1

Start in front stance with your left leg forward.

2

Step forward and punch to head level, jodan oi-zuki, with your right hand.

3

Without stepping, reverse punch to stomach level, chudan gyaku-zuki, using your left hand.

4

Punch using your right hand to stomach level.

RISING BLOCK, REVERSE PUNCH
Age-uke, Gyaku-zuki

This combination chains together two moves. The two component techniques, the block and the punch, should still remain distinct. Make sure that you complete the block before starting the punch. Ensure that you pull back your hip on the block and push your hip forward on the reverse punch.

1

Start in front stance.

2

Step forward and block to head level with rising block, age-uke. Make sure your left hip is pulled back so that your body faces to the side and your right shoulder drives the technique forward.

3

Without stepping, reverse punch with your left hand to stomach level, chudan gyaku-zuki. Make sure that you rotate your body so that your left hip and shoulder drive the punch forward. You should aim to finish with your left shoulder farther forward than your right.

OUTSIDE BLOCK, REVERSE PUNCH
Soto-uke, Gyaku-zuki

This combination follows the same pattern as the rising block combination but substitutes the middle level block, soto-uke. The two component techniques, the block and the punch, should still remain distinct. Make sure that you complete the block before starting the punch. Ensure that you pull back your hip on the block and push your hip forward on the reverse punch.

1

Start in front stance with your right leg forward.

2

Step forward with your left leg and block to stomach level with outside block, soto-uke. Make sure your right hip is pulled back so that your body faces to the side and your left shoulder drives the technique forward.

3

Without stepping, reverse punch with your right hand to stomach level, chudan gyaku-zuki. Make sure that you rotate your body so that your right hip and shoulder drive the punch forward. You should aim to finish with your right shoulder further forward than your left.

INSIDE BLOCK, REVERSE PUNCH

Uchi-uke, Gyaku-zuki

This combination is very similar to the outside block, and the final positions are identical except that this block passes through your center-line from the inside, finishing slightly on the outside. Ensure that you pull your hip back on the block and push it forward on the reverse punch.

1

Start in front stance, right leg forward.

2

Step forward with your left leg and block to stomach level with inside block, uchi-uke. Make sure your left hip is pulled back so that your body faces to the side and your right shoulder drives the technique forward.

3

Without stepping, reverse punch with your right hand to stomach level, chudan gyaku-zuki. Make sure that you rotate your body so that your right hip and shoulder drive the punch forward. You should aim to finish with your right shoulder farther forward than your left.

DOUBLE-HANDED BLOCK
Morote-uke

This is the same as an inside block except that the blocking fist is followed by the other fist, which should finish by pushing just below the blocking elbow. It is often called an augmented or reinforced block, but this is misleading because the second hand does not actually augment the block. The term morote just means that both hands are used. When morote-uke is used in kata, it is often actually a throw or an arm lock.

1

Start in front stance.

2

Prepare by pulling both hands to your right hip, left fist on top of right.

3

Step into front stance while simultaneously blocking with your left hand and pushing with your right fist just below your left elbow. Your right fist should be rotated so that your palm faces up. Keep your right elbow down so that it touches your body.

SPEAR-HAND STRIKE

Nukite-uchi

The spear-hand strike is made by pointing the fingers and striking with the fingertips. This strike is effective when used against small, soft targets like the throat or the solar plexus. The fingers should be kept tense and together. The striking hand should move in a straight line to the target and should be angled in slightly (just like a stepping punch) so that it hits in line with the center of the body. In Heian Nidan, you practice the spear-hand strike in combination with a blocking motion so that the left hand finishes palm down under the right elbow. This movement is called a pressing block, osae-uke.

1

Start in back stance with your left leg forward.

2a

Push your weight forward onto your left leg so that you shift into a front stance. At the same time, perform pressing block, osae-uke, by pressing down with your left hand, palm down, in front of your stomach.

2b

Step forward with your right foot into front stance. Perform spear hand strike to stomach level by extending your right arm over the top of your left hand with your fingers extended to make the spear shape. Your right elbow should finish touching the top of your left hand. Make sure that you rotate your body so that your right hip and shoulder drive the strike forward. You should aim to finish with your right shoulder farther forward than your left.

BACKFIST STRIKE
Uraken-uchi

This technique is made by striking with the first two knuckles on the top of the fist. It should be done using a whipping action, snapping back your fist as soon as it has hit. This is one technique in karate where bending the wrist is necessary because this allows you to hit with the knuckles, rather than the fragile small bones on the back of the hand.

1

Start in front stance with your right leg forward.

2

Slide your left leg forward and prepare to strike with your left fist by bringing it up alongside the right side of your face. Point your left elbow at the target and reach forward with your right arm.

3

Step into front stance while simultaneously striking head level with the back of your fist.

4

Snap your attack back, bringing your left fist back to your chest, palm down.

HAMMER FIST STRIKE

Tetsui-uchi

This technique can also be called the bottom-fist strike because it is done by striking with the bottom of the fist. It is similar to the hammer fist strike introduced in Heian Shodan, but strikes horizontally.

1

Start in front stance with your right leg forward.

2

Slide your left leg forward and prepare to strike with your left hand. Point your left elbow at the target and reach forward with your right arm.

3

Step into side stance while simultaneously striking with the bottom of your fist at chest level.

STRIKING AREAS

Make sure that you use the correct area of the hand when employing the different strikes.

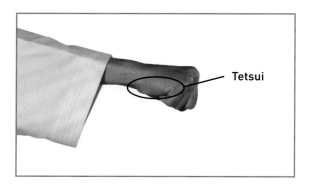

Tetsui

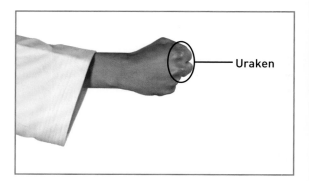

Uraken

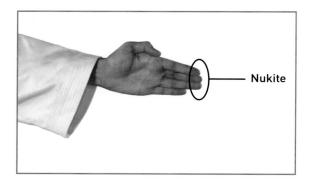

Nukite

Heian Nidan

This is the second kata in the Heian series of kata. Heian Nidan makes extensive use of back stance and knife-hand block. In fact, except for one technique, the first 16 moves are all performed in back stance. To perform this kata well, it is therefore imperative to ensure that your back stance is well formed, as described in the previous chapter.

KATA SEQUENCE

Bow. Announce kata "Heian Nidan" and step into ready stance, yoi-dachi.

This position, with both hands on the hip, is very common in shotokan karate and is sometimes called the "cup-and-saucer position."

1

Step out to the side with your left foot into back stance. While you do this, bring both hands to your right hip and then immediately throw a head level inside block, uchi-uke, to your left arm and a rising block, age-uke, with your right arm.

2

Sweep your left arm across your face and at the same time swing across your body in the opposite direction with a hammer fist strike using your right arm.

3

Hammer fist strike sideways with your left arm.

4

Pivot to face the other way. While you do this, bring both hands to your left hip and then immediately throw a head level inside block, uchi-uke, with your right arm and a rising block, age-uke, with your left arm.

73

5

Sweep your right arm across your face and at the same time swing across your body in the opposite direction with a hammer fist strike using your left arm.

6

Hammer fist strike sideways with your right arm.

7

Shift your left foot to your center and lift your right foot to your left knee. Place both fists on your left hip.

Side view.

8

Side rising kick with your right leg and backfist strike with your right hand.

9

Step down with your right foot into back stance with knife-hand block.

10

Step forwards with right-hand knife-hand block.

11

Step forwards with left-hand knife-hand block.

12

Block down with your left hand, palm down (osae-uke). Strike with a spear-hand, nukite, over the top with your right hand. Kiai.

13

Move your left foot and turn 270 degrees anti-clockwise into back stance, kokutsu-dachi, with left-hand knife-hand block, shuto-uke.

14

Step forwards, with your right foot at an angle of 45 degrees, into back stance with right-hand knife-hand block.

15

Move your right foot across into back stance with right-hand knife-hand block.

16

Step with your left foot at an angle of 45 degrees into back stance with left-hand knife-hand block.

Side view.

17

Move your left foot across and block with right-hand inside block.

Side view.

18

Without changing arm positions, front kick with your right leg.

Side view.

19

Step into front stance and punch with your left hand.

20

Without stepping, execute inside block with your left hand.

Side view.

21

Without changing arm positions, front kick with your left leg.

Side view.

22

Step into front stance and punch with your right hand.

Side view.

23

Step forwards into front stance and block with right-side morote-uke.

Side view.

24

Turn 270 degrees counter-clockwise by moving your left foot and execute left downward block.

25

Step using the right foot at an angle of 45 degrees and execute right rising block.

26

Turn 135 degrees clockwise by moving your right foot and execute right downward block.

27

Step using your left leg at an angle of 45 degrees and execute left rising block with kiai.

Finish by moving the left foot back into ready stance and bowing.

CHAPTER SIX yellow to green belt

At yellow belt level, you will be expected to be capable of switching smoothly between different types of stance. It is therefore important to understand the differences between the major stances, zenkutsu, kokutsu, and kiba-dachi. A common mistake is to fail to distinguish between the stances and to end up using some sort of hybrid stance throughout the yellow belt combinations or sections of the kata.

Syllabus Summary

Yellow belt gradings follow the following format:

YELLOW BELT GRADING SYLLABUS	
Basics	
Triple punch	Sanbon tsuki
Rising block, reverse punch, downward block	Age-uke, gyaku-zuki, gedan barai
Outside block, elbow strike	Soto-uke, empi-uchi
Inside block, reverse punch	Uchi-uke, gyaku-zuki
Knife-hand block, spear-hand strike	Shuto-uke, nukite-uchi
Consecutive front kicks	Mae ren-geri
Side thrusting kick	Yoko kekomi
Side rising kick	Yoko keage
Kata	
Heian Sandan	
Kumite	
One-step sparring	Ippon kumite
Head level stepping punch	Jodan oi-zuki
Stomach level stepping punch	Chudan oi-zuki

Basic Form

RISING BLOCK, REVERSE PUNCH, DOWNWARD BLOCK
Age-uke, Gyaku-zuki, Gedan Barai

Ensure that you pull back the opposite hip on the block and push that hip forward on the reverse punch. The hips should then be pulled back again on the final block. Try to make the first punch follow on quickly from the rising block and then leave a brief pause before the final block. The timing should then be: block, punch, pause, block.

Make sure that every individual technique is completed: do not make the rising block smaller in order to get to the punch quicker. Every individual technique should be done at the same speed. (Do not confuse this with the timing, which is concerned with the spaces between individual techniques rather than the techniques themselves.) A common mistake is to execute the first two techniques vigorously but then to move the hands slowly for the last block.

1

Start in front stance, zenkutsu-dachi.

2

Step forward and block to head level with rising block, age-uke.

3

Without stepping, reverse punch with your left hand to stomach level, chudan gyaku-zuki.

4

Without stepping, perform a lower sweeping block, gedan barai, with your right hand.

OUTSIDE BLOCK, ELBOW STRIKE
Soto-uke, Empi-uchi

Make sure that when you block, you are in front stance with the opposite hip pulled back. Use a big preparation for the elbow strike. When pulling back the front leg for the elbow strike preparation, ensure your movements remain dynamic by leaving your balance slightly forward. This means you can drive forward into the strike.

Do not make the mistake of merging the blocking action and the elbow striking action: there should be a distinct block in a good front stance. Make sure you complete this technique before going on to the elbow strike.

1

Start in front stance, zenkutsu-dachi.

2

Step forward into front stance, zenkutsu-dachi, and block to stomach level with outside block, soto-uke.

3

Slide your right foot back and prepare to strike by pulling your right hand back. Reach forward with your left hand.

4

Slide your right foot forward into side stance, kiba-dachi, and simultaneously execute right arm elbow strike, empi-uchi.

KNIFE-HAND BLOCK, SPEAR-HAND STRIKE
Shuto-uke, Nukite-uchi

Make sure that you step into back stance for the knife-hand block and then shift your weight forward into front stance for the spear-hand strike. You should complete the block before moving for the counterattack. A common mistake is to merge the two techniques, resulting in a weak block.

The retracted hand should remain open and finish on the solar plexus for the knife-hand block. For the spear-hand strike, your retracting hand should close into a fist and finish on the hip.

1

Start in back stance, kokutsu-dachi.

2

Step forward into back stance while simultaneously blocking with knife-hand block, shuto-uke.

3

Without stepping, push your right hip forward into front stance and execute spear-hand strike, nukite-uchi, with your right hand. Make sure that you rotate your body so that your right hip and shoulder drive the strike forward. You should aim to finish with your right shoulder farther forward than your left.

CONSECUTIVE FRONT KICKS

Mae Ren-geri

The two kicks in mae ren-geri should be done in quick succession (in "one breath"). Do not pause or even step into stance after the first kick. Both kicks are intended to be aimed at the same opponent, so be aware of the range of the two kicks. The first kick, which is a long reaching kick, is to stomach level. The step after this should be very short (step down just in front of the supporting foot) so that the head level kick, which is a short-range kick, reaches no farther than the first.

1 Start in front stance.

2 Front kick with your left leg to stomach level, chudan mae-geri.

3 Step down in a short stance.

4 Immediately kick with your right leg to head level, jodan mae-geri.

DOUBLE CROSSING BLOCK

This is the technique that characterizes the kata Heian Sandan (moves 2, 3, 5, and 6). It is more of a lock than a block, but it is simpler first to think of this as a blocking technique. The key to doing this technique well is to fold your arms so that your elbows are tight together and then to unfold your arms explosively. It will feel like your arms are going to collide, but don't worry—they won't. Try to make the movements as big and as bold as possible, blocking right across your body. Don't make the common mistake of simply waving your arms up and down without the folding action.

1

Start in ready stance.

2

Prepare by bringing your right fist alongside your left shoulder and your left fist to your right hip.

3

Perform downward block, gedan barai, with your right arm and inside block, uchi-uke, with your left arm. Try to get your arms to cross close together, with the downward block passing closer to your body than the inside block.

4

Now repeat: fold and unfold your arms. Imagine that someone has grabbed your left arm and that your right arm will knock their arm to your right and break their grip.

Heian Sandan

This is the third kata in the Heian series of kata. It contains examples of the yellow belt theme of switching between different stances. Attention must also be paid to this kata's signature moves: the double crossing block and the knee lifts. Heian Sandan is the first kata to make use of a sliding foot technique (yori-ashi), and this occurs in the last two moves of the kata.

KATA SEQUENCE

Bow. Announce kata 'Heian Sandan' and step into ready stance, yoi-dachi.

1

Step out to the side with your left foot into back stance. Perform stomach level inside block to the left.

2a

Move your right foot alongside your left foot and prepare to perform a double crossing block by bringing your right arm to your left hip and your left arm to your right shoulder.

2b

Straighten your legs and at the same time cross and uncross your arms, performing inside block with your right arm and downward block with your left arm.

3

Cross and uncross your arms, performing inside block with your left arm and downward block with your right arm.

4

Step with your right foot so you face the other way and perform a stomach level inside block to the side with your right arm.

5a

Move your left foot up alongside your right foot and prepare by crossing your left hand to your right hip and your right hand to your left shoulder.

5b

Straighten your legs and at the same time cross and uncross your arms, performing inside block with your left arm and downward block with your right arm.

6

Cross and uncross your arms, performing inside block with your right arm and downward block with your left arm.

7

Step out to your left with your left foot into back stance, kokutsu-dachi, and use double-handed block, morote-uke.

8

Block palm down with your left hand and strike over the top with spear-hand strike, nukite-uchi.

9

Move your left foot, rotating your body counterclockwise, step through into horse stance, kiba-dachi, and strike hammer fist, tetsui-uchi, with your left hand.

10

Step forward and punch with your right hand. Kiai.

11

Slowly, and with control, move your left foot toward the right into heisoku-dachi and rotate your body counterclockwise 180 degrees.

12a

Lift your right knee.

Side view.

12b

Twist your hip and stamp down with your right foot. Block to stomach level with your right elbow.

13

Throw a right-hand backfist strike, uraken-uchi, ensuring that your arm moves in the vertical plane so that your fist brushes past your shoulder. Snap your fist back to the hip following the same path.

14a

Lift your left knee.

14b

Twist your hip and stamp down with your left foot. Block to stomach level with your left elbow.

15

Perform a left hand backfist strike, uraken-uchi, ensuring that your arm moves in the vertical plane so that your fist brushes past your shoulder. Snap your fist back to your hip following the same path.

16a

Lift your right knee.

16b

Twist your hip and stamp down with your right foot. Block to stomach level with your right elbow.

17

Perform a right backfist strike, uraken-uchi, ensuring that your arm moves in the vertical plane. Snap your fist back to your hip following the same path.

18a

Block to the right side with vertical knife-hand.

Side view.

18b

Immediately step forward with your left foot and execute stepping punch.

Side view.

19a

Bring your right foot up alongside your left.

19b

Move your left foot around behind you and then out to the side, turning 180 degrees counterclockwise. Bring your left fist to your hip and your right fist over your left shoulder.

20

Slide to the right and move your right foot then your left foot, yori ashi. Bring your right fist to your hip and your left fist over your right shoulder. Kiai.

Finish by moving your left foot across into ready stance and bowing.

Basic One-Step Sparring

Kihon Ippon Kumite

Basic one-step sparring, kihon ippon kumite, is quite similar to gohon kumite, except that there is only one attack and counterattack before the exchange is stopped. The defender must respond with a counterattacking technique after every block. This may be a technique of the defender's own choice, but the simplest (and hence most reliable) counter-attack is the reverse punch.

In one-step sparring, the attacker should perform the head level attack followed by the stomach level attack using right-hand side attacks as illustrated in Chapter 3, with the defender using the left hand to block. The attacker then continues to do the same attacks using left-hand side attacks with the defender using the right hand to block.

Double crossing block drills

The double crossing block at the beginning of Heian Sandan is difficult to master. These drills are not intended as fighting applications but can be used to learn the correct path of the movements.

WRIST GRAB DRILL

When you perform the Heian Sandan double block, the downward block should travel closer to the body than the gedan barai. To help you do this, get your training partner to grab your wrist. When you perform the double block, the grabbing hand should get swept off your wrist by the inside block motion of your other arm. This will work only if you have the downward block motion traveling close to your body and the inside block passing farther away.

1

Perform inside block with your right hand and downward block with your left (Heian Sandan move 2). Your partner should grab your right wrist with his left hand.

2

Pull your right hand back as much as you can toward your left shoulder and move your left fist to your right hip.

3

Perform inside block with your left arm sweeping your partner's hand off your right wrist. Perform downward block with your right hand.

4

Now repeat with your partner grabbing your left wrist with his left hand.

BACKFIST DRILL

When performing the double crossing block it is easy to think of it as acting only sideways. However, if done correctly, it will also have a component of its motion that is directed forward. This motion can be used to strike with the back of the hand. This drill is to hone the use of this technique as a backfist strike. The trick is to pull your fists close to your body on the preparation phase so that they travel forward as well as sideways as you complete the technique. You can use focus pads to practice this drill but if you don't have any then you can use your partner's open hand as a target.

1

Perform inside block with your left hand and downward block with your right (Heian Sandan move 5). Your partner should place his open hand on your left knuckle.

2

Pull your left fist back to your right shoulder and right fist back to your left hip.

3

Perform the double block, striking your opponent's open hand with your right fist.

4

Repeat, striking the palm with your left fist.

CHAPTER **SEVEN** green to purple belt

The green belt syllabus introduces the roundhouse kick, mawashi-geri, that has become so popular in free-style sparring. A green belt is expected to be able to use kicks in sparring, and this, along with the athletically demanding kata Heian Yondan, means that the green belt level requires good flexibility.

Syllabus Summary

Green belt gradings follow the following format:

GREEN BELT GRADING SYLLABUS	
Basics	
Triple punch	Sanbon tsuki
Rising block, reverse punch, downward block	Age-uke, gyaku-zuki, gedan barai
Outside block, elbow strike, backfist strike	Soto-uke, empi-uchi, uraken-uchi
Inside block, jabbing punch, reverse punch	Uchi-uke, kizami-zuki, gyaku-zuki
Knife-hand block, jabbing front kick, spear-hand strike	Shuto-uke, kizami mae-geri, nukite-uchi
Consecutive front kicks	Mae ren-geri
Side thrusting kick	Yoko kekomi
Side rising kick	Yoko keage
Roundhouse kick	Mawashi-geri
Kata	
Heian Yondan	
Kumite	
One-step sparring	Ippon kumite
Head level stepping punch	Jodan oi-zuki
Stomach level stepping punch	Chudan oi-zuki
Front kick	Mae-geri
Side thrusting kick	Yoko kekomi

Basic Form

OUTSIDE BLOCK, ELBOW STRIKE, BACKFIST STRIKE
Soto-uke, Empi-uchi, Uraken-uchi

Make sure that the block is performed to completion. A common mistake is to rush from the block to the next move, resulting in a weak blocking technique. Conversely, try to use the momentum of the body while executing the elbow strike to fire off the backfist strike. The correct timing for the combination should be block, pause, elbow strike, backfist strike. The backfist strike should be done with a whipping action.

1

Start in front stance, zenkutsu-dachi.

2

Step forward and block to stomach level with outside block, soto-uke.

3

On the spot, shift your weight into side stance, kiba-dachi, and strike with your elbow, empi-uchi.

4

Now repeat with your partner grabbing your left wrist with his left hand.

5

Snap back your fist.

INSIDE BLOCK, JABBING PUNCH, REVERSE PUNCH

Uchi-uke, Kizami-zuki, Gyaku-zuki

As with the previous technique, make sure that the block is performed to completion. A common mistake is to rush from the block to the next move, resulting in a weak blocking technique. When punching with the leading hand, try to use as much of the body as possible to generate power and not just the arm. A good timing to use is block, pause, punch, punch.

1

Start in front stance, zenkutsu-dachi, with your right leg forwards.

2

Step forwards with your left leg and perform a stomach level inside block, uchi-uke.

3

Without stepping, punch using your left hand, kizami-zuki.

4

Without stepping, reverse punch, gyaku-zuki, with your right hand. Make sure that you rotate your body so that your right hip and shoulder drive the punch forward. You should aim to finish with your right shoulder further forward than your left.

KNIFE-HAND BLOCK, JABBING FRONT KICK, SPEAR-HAND STRIKE
Shuto-uke, Kizami Mae-geri, Nukite-uchi

Make sure that the block is performed to completion and in the correct stance. When kicking, try not to bring your body weight back more than necessary. If you can leave your weight forward, you will be able to make a fast transition and transfer power to the spear-hand strike.

1

Start in back stance, kokutsu-dachi.

2

Step forward into back stance and perform a stomach level knife-hand block, shuto-uke.

3

Without stepping, lift your front leg and execute front kick, mae-geri.

4

Without stepping, shift your body weight forward and strike to stomach level with spear-hand strike, nukite-uchi.

ROUNDHOUSE KICK

Mawashi-geri

The basic roundhouse kick should be done with as big a rotation as possible. Make sure that, when rotating, you pivot your supporting foot. Failure to do this will put an unnecessary strain on your ankle and will reduce the power of your kick. Traditionally, the striking area is the ball of the foot, but it is more common to use the shin. For sparring you should use the instep instead, because this allows you to control the delivery of the kick so as to avoid injuring your sparring partner. For self-defense applications, the roundhouse kick can be targeted almost anywhere including the face, floating ribs, stomach, thigh, or knees. For competitive sparring, the targets are usually limited to the head and torso above the belt.

1
Start in free-style front stance.

2
Lift your rear leg.

3
Swing your hips around so that you rotate on your supporting leg and execute roundhouse kick, mawashi-geri.

4
Snap back your kicking foot.

5
Step forward into front stance.

CROSS BLOCK
Juji-uke

The literal translation of juji-uke is "figure ten block" (the Japanese kanji character for the number ten is a cross) but it is more commonly called cross block. This technique can be performed to low level or head level. You should initially practice the low level version.

1

Start in front stance, zenkutsu-dachi.

2

Raise both the fists to your right shoulder with your right fist on top. Make sure that you lift your right elbow and drop your left.

3

Step forward into front stance and block down, as if blocking left-hand gedan barai and punching with your right hand. Get into a really low stance but keep your upper body upright.

KNIFE-HAND STRIKE

Shuto-uchi

The strike should be with the fleshy base of the hand with the palm up. It should be delivered in a tight circular path. This can be a very powerful attack if you can coordinate the arm movement with the rotation of your hips. You should feel like you are throwing a ball. The motion should start from your legs, then transmit to your hips, your shoulder, and finally to your elbow and hand.

1

Start in front stance, zenkutsu-dachi.

2

Prepare to strike with your left hand by pulling it back. Reach forward with your right hand.

3

Strike to head level with knife-hand strike, shuto-uchi.

WEDGE BLOCK
Kakiwake-uke

The literal translation of kakiwake-uke is "dividing apart reception" but is usually called wedge block. Probably it should really be called wedge defense because it doesn't block so much as break grabbing attacks by wedging them open.

1

Start in ready stance.

2

Bring both fists to your hips.

3

Slowly start to step forwards while crossing your arms in front of your body, palm sides facing in.

4

Step out into back stance and slowly open your arms and rotate so that the palm sides faces out.

Kakiwake-uke, close-up view.

Heian Yondan

This is the fourth kata in the Heian series. Heian Yondan is the most athletically challenging of the Heian kata, and contains no fewer than five kicks, which require leg flexibility to both the front and the side. This kata also makes extensive use of both slow and fast techniques. Demonstrating a good contrast between these techniques is critical to performing this kata well.

KATA SEQUENCE

Bow. Announce the kata "Heian Yondan" and step into ready stance.

1

Step out to the side with your left foot into back stance, kokutsu-dachi. With open hands, slowly raise your arms, performing upper-level inside block with your left arm and rising block with your right.

2

Pivot into back stance facing the other way. With open hands, slowly raise your arms, performing head level inside block with your right arm and rising block with your left.

3

Step to your left and perform a lower level cross-block, gedan juji-uke.

4

Step forwards into back stance, kokutsu-dachi, and perform a right-side double-handed block, morote-uke.

5

Pull your left leg up to your right knee, place both fists on your right hip and look to the left.

101

6

Kick to the left side with side rising kick, yoko keage, and simultaneously perform a left backfist strike, uraken-uchi.

7

Snap your foot back (but leave your left hand) and step down into front stance. Simultaneously, open the left hand and strike into it with your right elbow, empi-uchi. When you do this, you should pull your open hand back at the same time that you turn in with your elbow. However, the feeling should be more that the elbow is striking the hand than the other way around.

8

Shift your left foot halfway towards your right and then lift your right foot onto your knee. Place both fists on your left hip and look to the right.

9

Kick to the right side with a side rising kick, yoko keage, and simultaneously strike with right backfist strike, uraken-uchi.

10

Snap your foot back (but leave your right hand out) and step down into front stance. Simultaneously, open your right hand and strike into it with your left elbow, empi-uchi. When you do this, you should pull your open hand back at the same time that you turn in with your elbow. However, the feeling should be more that the elbow is striking the hand than the other way around.

11a

Using open hands, block to lower level with your left and upper level with your right.

11b

Using open hands, block to upper level with your left and strike knife-hand to head level, jodan shuto-uchi, with your right hand.

12a

Kick stomach level front kick, mae-geri chudan, with your right foot.

Side view

12b

Snap the leg back and simultaneously reach forwards with your left hand in a pressing block while lifting your right fist above your head.

Side view

12c

Both hands keep moving in a circular motion so that your left fist comes to your left hip and your right hand performs a backfist strike, uraken-uchi, while stepping forwards into crossed leg stance, kosa-dachi. Kiai.

13

Using a slow and controlled movement, pivot 135 degrees counter-clockwise and cross your arms, palms towards you, with your left arm on the outside. Open your arms, rotating your wrists out into wedge block, kakiwake-uke, and step out with your left leg into back stance.

14

Front kick to head level, jodan mae-geri, with your right leg.

15

Step down into front stance and immediately punch to stomach level, chudan oi-zuki, with your right fist.

16

Punch to stomach level, chudan gyaku-zuki, with your left fist.

17

Using a slow and controlled movement, pivot 90 degrees clockwise and pull your right foot back to your left. Simultaneously, cross your arms, palms towards you, with your right arm on the outside. Step out again with your right foot into back stance, kokutsu-dachi, and at the same time, open your arms, rotating the wrists out into wedge block, kakiwake-uke.

18

Perform head level front kick, jodan mae-geri, with your left leg.

19

Step down into front stance and immediately punch to stomach level, chudan oi-zuki, with your left fist.

20

Punch to stomach level, chudan gyaku-zuki, with your right fist.

21

Step 45 degrees to the left into back stance and use double-handed block, morote-uke, with the left side.

22

Step and use double-handed block, morote-uke, with the right side.

23

Step and use double-handed block, morote-uke, with the left side.

24

Move forwards into front stance and push your open hands up to head level, palms facing each other as if grabbing someone's head.

Side view.

25

Thrust your right knee upwards while simultaneously closing your fists and pulling them down to the level of your knee. Kiai.

Side view.

26

Pivot counter-clockwise to face towards the rear and step forwards with your left leg into back stance with a left knife-hand block, shuto-uke.

27

Step forwards with your right
foot into back stance with a
knife-hand block, shuto-uke.

Finish by moving your right
foot back into ready stance
and bowing.

Basic One-Step Sparring

FRONT KICK ATTACK
Mae-geri

When defending against a front kick, it is not sufficient to simply step back and block. Trying to block a powerful front kick using brute force could result in a broken arm. It is therefore important that the defender makes use of lateral motion and steps off the line of the attack using the blocking motion to deflect the kick. This avoids the danger inherent in trying to block a powerful technique, like a front kick, head on. Your blocking arm should be making contact with the side of the kicking leg, or even the underside, but certainly not the front edge. Moreover, stepping off the line of attack moves you into a flanking position, opening up greater opportunities for an effective counterattack. In addition, directing a block under an opponent's leg when they kick presents an opportunity to catch their leg.

1

Both the attacker and defender start in ready position. The attacker steps back right side with a downward block, gedan barai, then relaxes the hands to free-style fighting position and announces the attack: "Mae-geri!"

2

The attacker performs a right-leg front kick to the body with kiai. The defender steps back and to the right and blocks with a downward block, gedan barai.

3

The defender immediately counter-attacks with reverse punch. Kiai. The attacker withdraws, and, as he does so, the defender steps up, both finishing in yoi position.

SIDE THRUSTING KICK ATTACK
Yoko Kekomi

Similar to the defense against the front kick, the defender must step off the line of the attack when faced with a side thrusting kick. However, because of the trajectory of the side thrusting kick, this is most successful when stepping to the outside of the attacker.

1

Both the attacker and defender start in ready position. The attacker steps back right side with a downward block, gedan barai, and then relaxes the hands into free-style fighting position and announces the attack: "Yoko kekomi!"

2

The attacker kicks with a right-leg side thrusting kick to the body with a kiai. The defender steps back and to the left and blocks with an outside block, soto-uke.

3

The defender immediately counterattacks with reverse punch with a kiai. The attacker withdraws and, as he does so, the defender steps up, both finishing in ready stance, yoi-dachi.

CHAPTER **EIGHT** purple to purple and white belt

The syllabus between green belt and purple belt changes little, and so this is a good grade to try to perfect all the techniques that have gone before. The purple belt kata, Heian Godan, completes the Heian series of kata and this is an ideal time to ensure that all the Heian kata are known and understood.

Syllabus Summary

Purple belt gradings follow the following format:

PURPLE BELT GRADING SYLLABUS	
Basics	
Triple punch	Sanbon tsuki
Rising block, reverse punch, downward block	Age-uke, gyaku-zuki, gedan barai
Outside block, elbow strike, backfist strike, reverse punch	Soto-uke, empi-uchi, uraken-uchi, gyaku-zuki
Inside block, jabbing punch, reverse punch	Uchi-uke, kizami-zuki, gyaku-zuki
Knife-hand block, jabbing front kick, spear-hand strike	Shuto-uke, kizami mae-geri, nukite-uchi
Consecutive front kicks	Mae ren-geri
Side thrusting kick	Yoko kekomi
Side rising kick	Yoko keage
Roundhouse kick	Mawashi-geri
Kata	
Heian Godan	
Kumite	
One-step sparring	Ippon kumite
Head level stepping punch	Jodan oi-zuki
Stomach level stepping punch	Chudan oi-zuki
Front kick	Mae-geri
Side thrusting kick	Yoko kekomi

Basic Form

OUTSIDE BLOCK, ELBOW STRIKE, BACKFIST STRIKE, REVERSE PUNCH

Soto-uke, Empi-uchi, Uraken-uchi, Gyaku-zuki

Ensure that you use the momentum of the body while executing the elbow strike to fire off the backfist strike. Snap the fist straight back to the hip while punching with the other hand. Try to keep the arm muscles relaxed so that you get a whipping action on the backfist strike. Rotating the hips strongly will pull the backfist back to the hip and simultaneously fire the reverse punch effectively.

1

Start in front stance, zenkutsu-dachi.

2

Step forwards and block to stomach level with outside block, soto-uke.

3

On the spot, shift your weight into side stance, kiba-dachi, and strike with the elbow, empi-uchi.

4

Strike with backfist, uraken-uchi.

5

Shift into front stance and reverse punch, gyaku-zuki.

SWASTIKA BLOCK
Manji-uke

The swastika block, or swastika position, manji gamae, can be described simply as a downward sweeping block, gedan barai, with one hand and a simultaneous head level inside block, jodan uchi-uke, with the other hand. It is, however, a far more complex movement than that suggests, and it can be used as a throwing action or a grasping/pulling action combined with a strike.

1 Start in front stance, zenkutsu-dachi.

2 Step forward and block open-handed across the face with your left hand. This is known as sweeping block, nagashi-uke. Simultaneously, strike to low level with right knife-hand, shuto-uchi.

3 Close the fists and pull with the right hand so that it goes behind your head, with the palm facing toward you. Simultaneously, block down, gedan barai, with the left hand.

The Swastika

The swastika has existed as a religious symbol for thousands of years. For Hindus, it symbolizes well-being and good luck, and it is Sanskrit, the ancient ceremonial language of the Hindu religion, which gives us the word swastika, "su" meaning good and "vasti" meaning being. In Buddhist art and literature—as shown here—it is called a manji and represents universal harmony, the balance of opposites. It was not until the twentieth century, when the symbol was adopted by Adolf Hitler's Nazi party, that the symbol acquired negative connotations.

CRESCENT KICK, ELBOW STRIKE
Mikazuki-geri, Empi-uchi

Literally translated, mikazuki means "crescent moon" and describes the crescent-shaped path that the kick follows. When doing the crescent kick, hold your shoulder and elbow back until your foot strikes the target, then strongly rotate your hip forward so that your elbow strike is powerful. To increase the power of the kick and speed of the combination, aim your kick so that its highest point is above the height of the target. This ensures that it is moving downward as it makes contact, which will have the effect of reducing the delay between the kick and the subsequent elbow strike.

1

Start in front stance, zenkutsu-dachi.

2

Reach forward with an open hand.

3

Swing your leg around, keeping the leg relatively straight, and kick into your open hand. Make sure that you keep your open hand as steady as you can. Do not drop your hand so that you can get away with a lower kick. Equally, you shouldn't be pulling the target onto your foot. Instead your foot will have to travel to the target.

4

Immediately rotate your hip forward and strike with your elbow, empi-uchi, into your open hand, and land in horse stance, kiba-dachi. Ensure that the elbow is striking the hand rather than your hand slapping your elbow. Just as with the crescent kick, you shouldn't feel that you are pulling the target into your elbow. Just keep your hand still and hit it with your elbow.

HOOK PUNCH

Kagi Zuki

The simplest interpretation of the hook punch is a close-range punch that travels around, hitting the target from the side.

1

Start with your right hand on your hip and with your left arm reaching forward.

2

Push your right fist forward as if doing a straight punch to stomach level. Pull your left hand back to your left hip.

3

The right fist curves to the side to complete a hook punch, kagi zuki.

Alternatively, the hook punch action can be used to apply a lock. When applying the lock, the retracting hand is used to pull the opponent's arm and the leading hand is used to apply pressure to the opponent's elbow. You should practice this move as a slow controlled movement.

1

The attacker starts in front stance with the left leg forward.

2

The attacker steps and punches with his right hand. Use the soto-uke preparation position to block and grab with your right hand.

3

Use the soto-uke motion to strike your opponent's elbow.

4

Use a left-hand hook punch action to apply a lock. Shorten your stance by sliding your right foot forward.

Heian Godan

This is the fifth kata in the Heian series of kata. It is characterized primarily by its jumping technique, but it is also important for introducing the manji-uke, which is common in the advanced shotokan kata. Heian Godan also contains sequences that are used in the popular advanced kata, Bassai Dai, which is needed for grading to black belt. Heian Godan thus provides useful preparation for this important kata, but it can also lead to confusion for brown belts because a lapse in concentration can result in inadvertently crossing over into Bassai Dai which contains a similar sequence. For this reason, Heian Godan is popular with grading examiners in brown belt and black belt examinations.

KATA SEQUENCE

Bow. Announce the kata "Heian Godan" and step into ready stance.

1

Step with your left leg into back stance, kokutsu-dachi. Perform an inside block, uchi-uke, with your left arm.

2

Immediately punch with your right hand, gyaku-zuki, remaining in back stance.

3

Slowly bring your right foot alongside your left, while simultaneously bringing your left arm into a hook punch position, kagi zuki.

4

Step with your right leg into back stance, kokutsu-dachi. Perform an inside block, uchi-uke, with your left arm.

5

Immediately punch with your left hand, gyaku-zuki, remaining in back stance.

6

Slowly bring your left foot alongside your right, while simultaneously bringing your right arm into a hook punch position, kagi zuki.

7

Step forward with your right leg into back stance, kokutsu-dachi, while blocking with double-handed block, morote-uke.

8

Step forward into front stance, zenkutsu-dachi, and block with lower level cross-block, gedan juji-uke.

9a

Pull your hands back to your stomach and open your hands.

9b

Block to head level with open-handed cross-block, jodan juji-uke.

10

Bring your hands down to the right side of your body just above the belt. They should rotate as they move so they finish with palms together, left on top of right.

11

Without stepping, punch with your left hand.

12

Stepping punch with your right hand. Kiai.

Side view

13

Turn to face the opposite direction by looking back over your left shoulder and then rotating anti-clockwise, pivoting on your left foot. Step through, lifting your right knee and stamping down while simultaneously blocking down with your right hand, gedan barai.

Side view

14

Slowly cross your arms, right over left. Open your arms slowly and smoothly, blocking with the back of your open hand.

15

Crescent kick with your right leg into your open hand.

Side view.

16

Immediately strike into your left palm with your right elbow, while stepping down into side stance, kiba-dachi.

17

Look to the right and use double-handed block, morote-uke, while moving your left foot into crossed leg stance, kosa-dachi.

18

Upper-cut with your right fist, keeping your left fist on the forearm, and look behind you while moving your left foot into a very short back stance. This technique is sometimes referred to as double handed rear rising punch, morote koho tsuki-age. Your left foot should be making very light contact with the floor with your heel slightly off the ground. Almost all your weight should be on your right foot.

Side view

19a

Jump by lifting first your right knee and then your left and rotating 180 degrees. Bring your fists to your hip. Kiai.

19b

Land in crossed leg stance, kosa-dachi, and bring your fists down in a low level cross block, gedan juji-uke. Keep your back straight and regain your balance briefly before proceeding to the next step.

20

Step to the right into front stance and use double-handed block, morote-uke.

21

Look over your left shoulder and turn 180 degrees into front stance, while blocking across your face, nagashi-uke, with open left hand. Strike to the lower level with right-side knife-hand strike, gedan shuto-uchi.

22

Switch into back stance, kokutsu-dachi, by shifting your weight onto your right foot. Simultaneously, execute swastika block, manji-uke, by pulling your right hand.

Side view

23

Slowly pull your left foot to your right and straighten your legs.

24

Step forward with your right foot into front stance, while blocking across your face, nagashi-uke, with open right hand and strike to the lower level with left-side knife-hand strike, gedan shuto-uchi.

25

Shift your weight back into back stance, kokutsu-dachi, with swastika block, manji-uke, by pulling your left hand.

Finish by moving your right foot back into ready stance and bowing.

JUMPING IN HEIAN GODAN

This is a breakdown of how to do the jump, move 19, from Heian Godan. The jump should be done smoothly and quickly. The objective is to jump upward rather than across, though there is still some lateral movement. This upward motion should be achieved more by lifting and tucking the legs than by raising the center of mass.

1

Start in short, high back stance with your right arm lifted, left fist on the forearm (Heian Godan step 18).

2

Rotate by lifting your right knee to your chest. Bring your fists to your hips.

3

Lift your left leg and tuck your left ankle on top of your right ankle. This move should flow uninterrupted from the previous one so that you continue to rotate in mid-air.

4

Land in crossed leg stance with the left foot behind your right foot, and block down with cross block, juji-uke. Make sure your back is straight.

NAGASHI-UKE DRILL

Nagashi-uke, sweeping block, is sometimes called flowing block because the idea is to deflect an incoming attack and then to flow past it. The nagashi-ukes in Heian Godan are often misunderstood, and it is unfortunately too easy to shortcut the block and render it useless.

Use this drill to practice the steps 21 through to 24 in Heian Godan. This is not intended to be a fighting application of the moves but is simply a way of practicing the correct path of the nagashi-uke. Your partner should hold a static position with his fist held out for you to push to the side. As you deflect the punch, you should flow past it, moving in close enough to deliver a knife-hand strike.

1

Start facing away from your partner in front stance with your hands in the morote-uke position (Heian Godan step 20). Your partner stands behind you with his fist out at head height.

2

Let your left arm drop and then swing round behind you as you start to turn. Lift your right hand up to head height ready to deliver a knife-hand strike, shuto-uchi.

3

Your left arm travels under your partner's fist then curves up. As you turn to face your partner, bring your left arm back over to your right, sweeping your partner's punching hand out of the way with nagashi-uke.

4

Swing your right hand down to your partner's leg, making light contact with knife-hand strike (Heian Godan step 21). If you find that you are unable to reach, then you need to push forward into a longer, lower stance. Be careful not to lean forward by bending from the waist. You still need to stay upright.

5

Perform manji-uke
(Heian Godan step 22)

6

Pull your front foot back
(Heian Godan step 23).
Your partner resets his fist
position, aiming it again at
your head. Bring your left
hand up to the left at head
height ready to deliver a
knife-hand strike,
shuto-uchi.

7

Step forward with your
right foot and use your
right hand to deflect
your partner's fist to the
left.

8

Swing your left hand down to
your partner's leg, making
light contact with knife-hand
strike (Heian Godan step 24).

CHAPTER **NINE** purple and white to brown belt

Purple and white belt represents the last of the intermediate grades and is the gateway to the advanced grades of brown belt and beyond. Beyond this grade, the syllabus is very different. It's therefore important for the purple and white belt student to perfect their set of techniques so that they are ready to move on to new things. Students at this grade should make a special effort to perfect the focus (kime) of their techniques. This is a very important aspect of karate training and one that is especially crucial for the purple and white belt kata, Tekki Shodan.

Syllabus Summary

Purple and white belt gradings follow the following format:

PURPLE AND WHITE BELT GRADING SYLLABUS	
Basics	
Triple punch	Sanbon tsuki
Rising block, reverse punch, downward block	Age-uke, gyaku-zuki, gedan barai
Outside block, elbow strike, backfist strike, reverse punch, downward block	Soto-uke, empi-uchi, uraken-uchi, gyaku-zuki, gedan barai
Inside block, jabbing punch, reverse punch, downward block	Uchi-uke, kizami-zuki, gyaku-zuki, gedan barai
Knife-hand block, jabbing front kick, spear-hand strike	Shuto-uke, kizami mae-geri, nukite-uchi
Consecutive front kicks	Mae ren-geri
Side thrusting kick	Yoko kekomi
Side rising kick	Yoko keage
Roundhouse kick	Mawashi-geri
Back kick	Ushiro-geri
Kata	
Tekki Shodan	
Kumite	
One-step sparring	Ippon kumite

Head level stepping punch	**Jodan oi-zuki**
Stomach level stepping punch	**Chudan oi-zuki**
Front kick	**Mae-geri**
Side thrusting kick	**Yoko kekomi**
Roundhouse kick	**Mawashi-geri**

Basic Form

OUTSIDE BLOCK, ELBOW STRIKE, BACKFIST STRIKE, REVERSE PUNCH, DOWNWARD BLOCK

Soto-uke, Empi-uchi, Uraken-uchi, Gyaku-zuki, Gedan Barai

Ensure that no techniques are lost in this long combination. The first block must be strong with good focus (kime). Use natural flow to make the best use of your momentum for the next three moves, while keeping each move large and distinct. Ensure that the last move is as strong as all the others. A good timing to use is block, pause, strike, strike, punch, pause, block.

1

Start in front stance, zenkutsu-dachi.

2

Step forward and perform a stomach level outside block, soto-uke.

3

On the spot, shift your weight into side stance, kiba-dachi, and strike with your elbow, empi-uchi.

4

Strike with backfist, uraken-uchi.

5

Shift into front stance and throw reverse punch, gyaku-zuki.

6

Downward block, gedan barai.

125

INSIDE BLOCK, JABBING PUNCH, REVERSE PUNCH, DOWNWARD BLOCK
Uchi-uke, Kizame-zuki, Gyaku-zuki, Gedan Barai

1

Start in front stance, zenkutsu-dachi.

2

Step forward and perform stomach level outside block, uchi-uke.

3

Without stepping, punch using your leading hand, kizame-zuki.

4

Without stepping, reverse punch, gyaku-zuki.

5

Downward block, gedan barai.

RETURNING WAVE KICK
Nami Gaeshi-geri

The returning wave kick is a short lifting kick that moves in a short arc. It can be used as a tripping attack and is the basis for leg sweeps, ashi barai, which are common in free-style sparring. You can practice this kick in side stance using your own hands as a target.

1 Start in side stance, kiba-dachi. Make a target by placing your hands, palms down, at hip height.

2 Without shifting your weight, lift your foot and strike your hands using the bottom of your foot.

COMMON MISTAKES

Don't kick the opposite leg

Don't shift your balance onto the grounded leg; instead kick faster and keep your body weight low

BACK KICK
Ushiro-geri

It is important to kick along your center-line. In this regard, it is similar to the front kick. Ensure that the recoil is as strong as the kick itself. This will help drive you forward into your next move (which in this case is just to return to fighting posture but is more commonly a punch). The striking surface for this kick is the heel. When used in karate sparring, it is initiated by spinning to face away from the opponent. For self-defense situations, it is less likely that you would want to do this but this kick would be appropriate if an opponent were to approach you from behind.

1
Start in free-style stance. Keep your weight on the balls of your feet. Use a narrow stance.

2
Move your left foot towards your right, rotating around your left hip. Your hips should move forwards.

3
Lift your foot, keeping your knee bent, ready to kick.

Side view

4
Kick by thrusting your leg back in a straight line. Make sure that you do not let your knee come out to the side. Your knee should pass under your body, brushing past your supporting leg, and your toes should point down at the end of the kick.

5
Recoil the leg along the line of the kick.

6
Step down.

COMMON MISTAKES

Incorrect path

The back kick is done all on one line. A common mistake is to let the leg swing out away from that line. To correct this, keep the knees together when starting the kick.

Incorrect form: the leg swings out

Correct form: the leg goes back in a straight line

Incorrect withdrawal

After kicking, a common mistake is to fail to pull the knee back. To correct this, focus on pulling the knee back along the path that the kick followed.

Incorrect form: the leg "hooks" back after the kick

Correct form: the leg pulled back by the retracting knee

129

Tekki Shodan

This is the first kata in the Tekki series of kata. The kanji for Tekki is made up of two characters, one meaning iron and the other meaning horse. It was originally called Naihanchi (and before that Naifanchi, using the Chinese pronunciation) and was introduced to Okinawa by Sokon Matsumura. Some stories say that he learned the kata in China, but this is by no means certain, and he may well have developed it himself. It was obviously a very important kata to the karate masters in Shuri—Itosu is said to have made Gichin Funakoshi practice Naihanchi for three years. This seems strange considering that Shuri-te, which shotokan is based on, is concerned primarily with linear strikes, and these signature moves are absent from Tekki Shodan.

The Heian Kata that precede Tekki Shodan are obviously from the same family, with moves that advance then change direction like they are chasing down and destroying enemies. Tekki Shodan is quite different. It stays in a fairly static horse stance, twisting and turning but staying very localized. Its use of horse stance throughout suggests that Tekki Shodan is designed for close-in combat, using grappling techniques and short range strikes. There are two other kata in the Tekki series, Tekki Nidan and Tekki Sandan, which are practiced by advanced students. They are very similar in style to Tekki Shodan, and together they are almost like an entire fighting system on their own.

When performing the kata, use the upper body to make the moves as big and as strong as possible while still maintaining a good side stance (kiba-dachi). It is essential that you use strong focused techniques to emphasize the strength of the arm movements.

KATA SEQUENCE
Bow. Announce the kata "Tekki Shodan."

Put your feet together. Place your left hand over your right with your fingertips touching.

1

Drop your weight slightly by bending your knees and step with your left foot in front of your right.

2a

Lift your right knee.

2b

Stamp down with your right foot landing in side stance, kiba-dachi, and simultaneously block with the back of your right hand to the right.

3

Pull back your right hand and elbow strike, empi-uchi, into it with your left elbow.

4

Pull both hands to your right hip, left on top of right (cup-and-saucer position), and look to the left.

5

Perform downward block, gedan barai, to the left with your left arm.

6

Throw hook punch, kagi zuki, to the left with your right hand.

7

Step across to the left with your right foot in front of your left.

8a

Lift your left knee.

8b

Stamp down with your left foot into kiba-dachi. At the same time, bring your right fist to the left shoulder and execute inside block, uchi-uke.

9a

Cross your arms, with your left arm on the outside. Straighten your right arm and bring your left hand up to the left side of your head performing an upper level sweeping block, jodan nagashi-uke.

9b

Perform backfist strike with your left hand and simultaneously bend your right arm, bringing your right hand under your left elbow.

10

Look to the left.

11a

Perform returning wave kick, nami gaeshi-geri, with your left foot.

11b

Swing your arms to the left, rotating your left palm away from you.

12

Look to the right.

13a

Perform returning wave kick, nami gaeshi-geri, with your right foot.

13b

Swing your arms to the right, rotating your left palm towards you.

14a

Bring your hands to your right hip, the left on top of the right (cup-and-saucer position), and look to the left.

14b

Throw left hand hammer fist strike and right hand hook punch, kagi zuki, to the left. Kiai.

15

Smoothly cross and open your arms with a continuous movement, blocking to the left with the back of your left hand.

16

Pull back your left hand and elbow strike, empi-uchi, into it with your right elbow.

17

Pull both hands to your left hip, right on top of left (cup-and-saucer position), and look to the right.

18

Perform downward block, gedan barai, to the right with your right arm.

19

Throw hook punch, kagi zuki, to the right with your left hand.

20

Step across to the right with your left foot in front of your right.

21a

Lift your right knee.

21b

Stamp down with your right foot into kiba-dachi. At the same time, bring your left fist to your right shoulder and execute inside block, uchi-uke.

22a

Cross your arms, with your right arm on the outside. Straighten your left arm and bring your right hand up on the right side of your head in upper level sweeping block, jodan nagashi-uke.

22b

Perform backfist strike with your right hand and simultaneously bend your left arm, bringing your left hand under your right elbow.

23

Look to the right.

24a

Perform returning wave kick, nami gaeshi-geri, with the right foot.

24b

Swing your arms to the right, rotating your right palm away from you.

25

Look to the left.

26a

Perform returning wave kick, nami gaeshi-geri, with the left foot.

26b

Swing your arms to the left, rotating your right palm toward you.

27a

Bring your hands to your left hip, the right on top of the left (cup-and-saucer position). Look to the right.

27b

Throw right-hand hammer fist strike and left-hand hook punch, kagi zuki, to the right. Kiai.

Finish by moving your right foot to the left and your left hand over your right hand with the fingertips touching. Bow.

Basic One-Step Sparring

ROUNDHOUSE KICK ATTACK
Mawashi-geri

1

Both the attacker and the defender start in the ready position. The attacker steps back with the right foot with a downward block, gedan barai, and then relaxes the hands to free-style fighting position and announces the attack: "Mawashi-geri!"

2

The attacker performs a right-leg roundhouse kick to the head with kiai. The defender steps back and to the right and blocks with an inside block, uchi-uke.

3

The defender immediately counterattacks using a reverse punch with kiai. The attacker withdraws and, as he does so, the defender steps up, both finishing in ready stance, yoi-dachi.

CHAPTER TEN brown to black belt

Upon reaching brown belt, you will now be considered a senior grade in your club, and, even though you have a lot to learn for black belt, lower grades will already be looking up to you to set standards and offer technical guidance.

At this level, there is a step change in the syllabus format. The basics will have more focus on kicking combinations, and on top of these new combinations you will still be expected to remember all the combinations you learned for previous gradings. You will also be expected to be able to pick up new combinations quickly and to perform them fluently.

The kata that you have to learn, Bassai Dai, is double the length of the previous kata and requires more study to learn and greater stamina to perform. There is also now a greater emphasis on sparring. From this point, you have about one year to train for black belt.

Syllabus Summary

Brown belt gradings (that is to say, grading to brown belt with a white stripe and grading to brown belt with two white stripes) follow the following format:

BROWN BELT GRADING SYLLABUS	
Basics	
Triple punch	Kizami-zuki, oi-zuki, gyaku-zuki
Front kick combination	Mae-geri, oi-zuki, gyaku-zuki
Side thrusting kick combination	Yoko kekomi, uraken-uchi, gyaku-zuki
Roundhouse kick combination	Mawashi-geri, uraken-uchi, gyaku-zuki
Back kick combination	Ushiro-geri, uraken-uchi, gyaku-zuki
Kata	
Bassai Dai	
Kumite	
One-step free sparring	Jiyu ippon kumite
Head level stepping punch	Jodan oi-zuki
Stomach level stepping punch	Chudan oi-zuki

Front kick	Mae-geri
Side thrusting kick	Yoko kekomi
Roundhouse kick	Mawashi-geri
Back kick	Ushiro-geri

In addition, when grading to black belt, you will be expected to demonstrate the following:

BLACK BELT GRADING SYLLABUS	
Basics	
Four-kick combination	Mae-geri, yoko kekomi, mawashi-geri, ushiro-geri, uraken-uchi, gyaku-zuki
Standing kicks	Mae-geri, yoko kekomi, ushiro-geri
Black belt combination	
Kata	
Choose one from:	
Bassai Dai, Kanku Dai, Jion, Empi, Hangetsu	
Kumite	
Free sparring	Jiyu-kumite

Fundamentals

When performing the brown belt basic form, remember the basic form from previous grades because it still applies. Do not abandon what you have learned before: really the only difference at this level is that you start and finish in free-fighting stance. This means that you should still endeavor to use low, long stances during the sequences and use big, fully completed techniques.

FIGHTING STANCE

Kamae

The fighting stance is not a formally defined stance, but consider the following:

- Point your front foot in the direction that you are going.

- Put your weight over your front foot and on the ball of the foot.

- Have your body turned to the side but your head turned to the front.

- Hold your hands up in a guard with your fists pointing at your target.

The fighting stance, kamae

Basic Form

TRIPLE PUNCH

The triple punch combination should be a continuous stream of punches. Try to keep pauses between the attacks to a minimum by pushing your weight forward over the front foot when doing the first punch. This has the effect of not only increasing the range and power of this punch but also of allowing the second punch, the stepping punch, to proceed more rapidly.

Each time you punch, you must pull back the opposite fist to your hip. This is important because it encourages a stronger, more committed punch and also allows a bigger, and therefore more powerful, motion on the next punch.
It is not just during the punching combination that you have to worry about pulling back the reverse hand. The same advice also applies to the kicking combinations. It is a common mistake throughout all the brown belt combinations to focus on the punching hand and leave the other hand "floating."

1
Start in fighting stance with your left leg forward.

2
On the spot, punch with your leading hand, kizame-zuki.

3
Stepping punch, oi-zuki.

4
Reverse punch, gyaku-zuki. Lock-out the technique briefly before returning to fighting stance, kamae.

FRONT KICK COMBINATION

When kicking with a front kick, you should not change your hand position. Only as you finish the kick and your foot touches the ground should you allow your arms to move as you unleash the punch. As with the triple punch combination, it is important to pull back the opposite hand when punching.

1
Start in fighting stance with your left leg forward.

2
Front kick, mae-geri, with your right foot.

3
As you land, punch with your right hand, oi-zuki.

4
Reverse punch with your left hand. Lock-out the technique briefly before returning to fighting stance, kamae.

SIDE THRUSTING KICK COMBINATION

When you kick with the side thrusting kick, ensure that you commit your hip. Remember to lock your kick in position because this is a thrust kick. Pull back your leg strongly: this will actually help you move forward faster for the next move.

Each time you kick, check that you are pushing your hip as much as you can. Failing to use your hip correctly will make the kick look weak and uncommitted.

1

Start in fighting stance with your left leg forward.

2

Side thrusting kick, yoko kekomi, with your right foot.

3

Backfist strike, uraken-uchi, with your right hand.

4

Reverse punch with your left hand. Lock-out the technique briefly before returning to fighting stance, kamae.

ROUNDHOUSE KICK COMBINATION

There are two ways of doing the roundhouse kick. The first is to try to swing the leg through the target. This way maximizes the power of the kick at the expense of range and is appropriate when practicing by kicking a bag or strike shield. The second way is to focus on range by pushing your hips forward toward the target and, rather than swinging through the target, instead snap the foot back. You should use this method when practicing kicking in the air or with a partner.

1

Start in fighting stance with your left leg forward.

2

Roundhouse kick, mawashi-geri, with your right foot.

3

Backfist strike, uraken-uchi, with your right hand.

4

Reverse punch with your left hand. Lock-out the technique briefly before returning to fighting stance, kamae.

BACK KICK COMBINATION

Sometimes you will be asked to do this combination without step 3, the backfist strike, and instead proceed straight to the reverse punch. You should be able to demonstrate this combination with or without the backfist strike.

1

Start in fighting stance with your left leg forward.

2

Back kick, ushiro-geri, with your right foot.

3

Backfist strike, uraken-uchi, with your right hand.

4

Reverse punch with your left hand. Lock-out the technique briefly before returning to fighting stance, kamae.

FOUR-KICK COMBINATION

1 Start in fighting stance with your left leg forward.

2 Front kick, mae-geri, with your right foot.

3 Side thrusting kick, yoko kekomi, with your left foot.

4 Roundhouse kick, mawashi-geri, with your right foot.

5 Back kick, ushiro-geri, with your left foot.

6 Backfist strike, uraken-uchi, with your left hand.

7 Reverse punch, gyaku-zuki, with your right hand. Lock-out the technique briefly before returning to fighting stance, kamae.

STANDING KICKS

Make sure that you regain balance between kicks. Trying to kick while off balance will result in a weak kick. With each kick, ensure that the path that your foot follows when you retract it is the same as the path it went out on.

1

Start in fighting stance with your left leg forward.

2

Front kick, mae-geri, with your right foot.

3

Snap back the kick keeping your knee raised ready for the next kick.

4

Without stepping down, do a side thrusting kick, yoko kekomi, to the right using the same foot. Remember that this thrusting kick should be held out briefly before you pull your foot back.

5

Retract your foot and return to the knee lifted position with your hips turned to the front again.

6

Without stepping down, back kick, ushiro-geri, with the same foot. Just like yoko kekomi, this is a thrusting kick and so should be held out briefly before you pull your foot back.

7

Return to fighting stance.

BLACK BELT COMBINATION

At black belt level, you will be expected to intermix techniques to form long combinations. The following combination is commonly asked for at black belt gradings.

1

Start in fighting stance with your left leg forward.

2

Front kick, mae-geri, with your right foot.

3

Punch with your right hand.

4

Reverse punch with your left hand.

5

Step back and perform left-side downward block, gedan barai.

6

Reverse punch with your right hand

7

Roundhouse kick, mawashi-geri, with your right foot.

8

Backfist strike, uraken-uchi, with your right hand.

9

Stepping punch, oi-zuki, with your left hand.

10

Immediately snap your fist back and return to fighting stance, kamae.

Bassai Dai

Bassai, originally called Passai in Okinawa, is most often translated as "storm a fortress." However, it is more likely that it means "extract from a fortress." Nobody really knows for sure what the name means but I like to think that, in view of Matsumura and Itosu's roles as bodyguards to the king, they would have had rescuing the king from Shuri Castle in mind when they practiced this kata.

The kanji Bassai Dai

There are many versions of Bassai (Masatoshi Nakayama estimated that there were hundreds), about 11 of which are still practiced today. In creating shotokan karate, Master Gichin Funakoshi selected the version he considered the most effective as one of the 15 core shotokan kata. This version of Bassai became referred to as Bassai Dai, distinguishing it from another well-known variation that is included in the shotokan system, termed Bassai Sho. Here Dai means big or major and Sho means small or minor, the implication being that the Dai version should be practiced first (being one of Funakoshi's 15 core kata), while the Sho version is considered only as an auxiliary.

Bassai Dai was demonstrated for the first time in Japan by Gichin Funakoshi in 1922. Today it is one of the most popular kata practiced throughout the various branches of karate and is often used as the main test kata for shodan (black belt) grading. It is twice the length of any of the individual kata that precede it (Heian series and Tekki Shodan), and it requires good physical fitness to perform from start to finish at full power.

KATA SEQUENCE
Bow. Announce the kata "Bassai Dai."

Put your feet together and clasp your right fist in your left hand.

1a

Swing your arms back to the left side and shift your weight forward ready to move. (Funakoshi added a knee-lift here, but this was later removed by Nakayama. Today both forms are followed.)

1b

Strike forward with the back of your right fist. Place your left hand on your right forearm. Simultaneously, leap forward with your right foot and tuck your left foot behind your right (crossed leg stance, kosa-dachi). This jumping movement should focus on traveling forward, rather than vertically. You should aim to travel about one and a half times as far as you normally step.

2

Turn to face the opposite direction by stepping back with your left foot so that you finish in front stance. Inside block, uchi-uke, with your left hand.

3

Without stepping, perform an inside block, uchi-uke with your right hand.

4

Turn and perform outside block, soto-uke with your left hand.

5

Without stepping, perform inside block, uchi-uke with your right hand.

6a

Bring your right foot back alongside your left while turning to your right. As you do this, sweep your right arm through in front of you, performing a low level scooping block, sukui uke.

6b

Continue the sweeping movement so that your hand moves all the way up to head height.

6c

Step forward into front stance with your right foot. Perform outside block, soto-uke, with your right hand.

7

Without stepping, perform inside block, uchi-uke with your left hand.

8

Rotate to your left, moving your left foot in so that you stand in a shoulder-width stance. As you do this, bring both fists to your right hip.

9

Using a slow, controlled movement, make a vertical knife-hand block, tate shuto-uke, with your left hand.

10

Without stepping, punch using your right hand.

11

Pull your right hand to your left shoulder and then continue the motion forward again, performing an inside block, uchi-uke, pivoting on the spot.

12

Straighten your hips and punch with your left hand.

13

Pull your left hand to your right shoulder. Perform inside block, uchi-uke, pivoting on the spot.

14

Step forward with your right leg into back stance and perform knife-hand block, shuto-uke.

15

Step forward with your left leg into back stance and perform knife-hand block, shuto-uke.

16

Step forward with your right leg into back stance and perform knife-hand block, shuto-uke.

17

Immediately step back with your right leg into back stance with knife-hand block, shuto-uke.

18

Shift into front stance while your right hand reaches up and catches. Pull your right hand back using grasping block, tsukami-uke.

19

Prepare to kick by lifting your right knee as high as you can and then immediately perform a low level side thrusting kick while pulling your fists up to your ribcage on the side of your body. Kiai.

20

Step into back stance with knife-hand block, shuto-uke.

21

Step forwards with your right leg into back stance with knife-hand block, shuto-uke.

22

Slowly move your right foot back to meet your left and raise both arms into a double rising block position, morote-age-uke.

23a

Abruptly pull your arms apart and shift your weight forwards onto your toes, ready to move.

Side view.

23b

Immediately step forwards with your right foot into front stance and strike at stomach level with scissors strike, hasami uchi, by swinging round with both fists in a double hammer fist strike, tetsui-uchi.

24

Immediately slide forwards and punch with your right fist, oi-zuki. To do this sliding motion correctly, first lift your front foot forward and drive forward by extending your rear leg. As your front foot lands, drag your rear leg forward slightly after you.

25

Turn and strike right knife-hand, shuto-uchi, while blocking open-handed across your face with your left hand.

26
Using a slow, steady movement draw your left foot back to the right while pulling your right fist up behind your head and blocking down slowly with your left, gedan barai.

Side view.

27
Lift your right knee high and stamp down into horse stance, kiba-dachi, and simultaneously perform downward block, gedan barai, with your left hand.

28
Look over your left shoulder and with a slow, steady motion, cross and uncross your arms, blocking open-handed to the left with the back of your hand while drawing your right hand back to your hip.

Side view.

29
Crescent kick, mikazuki-geri, with your right foot into your left hand. Make sure that you keep your right side back as much as you can with your fist on your hip and your elbow tucked in behind you. This means that you can maximise the power of the next move.

30
Elbow strike, empi-uchi, with your right elbow into your left hand. The power for this move is generated by turning your whole body into the attack. As you turn your body, land in horse riding stance.

Side view.

31
Punch down with your right hand, bringing your left fist up to the inside of your right elbow.

Side view.

32
Punch down with your left hand, bringing your right fist up to the inside of your left elbow.

33

Punch down with your right hand, bringing your left fist up to the inside of your right elbow.

Side view.

34

Bring both fists to your left hip and look to the right. Step out with your right foot into a narrow front stance and attack with both fists: right fist to stomach level, left fist over your head. This is known as a mountain punch, yama-zuki.

35

Slowly draw your right foot back to meet your left and bring both fists to your right hip. As you do this, rotate your upper body, pulling your left shoulder back and pushing your right shoulder forward.

36

Lift your left knee and step forward into front stance with mountain punch, yama-zuki: left fist to stomach level, right fist over your head.

37

Slowly draw your left foot back to meet your right and bring both fists to your left hip. As you do this, rotate your upper body, pulling your right shoulder back and pushing your left shoulder forward.

38

Lift your right knee and step forward into front stance with mountain punch, yama-zuki: right fist to stomach level, left fist over your head.

39a

Extend your right arm up and look over your left shoulder, pulling your left hand to your hip.

39b

Turn by moving your left foot counterclockwise and swing your right arm across your body in a scooping block, sukui-uke.

155

40a

Extend your left arm up above you.

40b

Pivot and swing your left arm across your body from left to right in a scooping block, sukui-uke. Finish with a closed fist, palm-side up.

41

Move your left foot to your center point. Then step forward at a 45-degree angle with your right foot. Finish in back stance with knife-hand block, shuto-uke.

42

Look over your left shoulder and then slowly move your right foot so that you rotate 90 degrees clockwise.

43

Step with your right foot to your center point. Then step forward with your left foot into back stance with knife-hand block, shuto-uke. Kiai.

Finish by slowly drawing your left foot back to your right and clasping your right fist in your left hand. Bow.

KATA DETAILS
Grasping Block, Side Thrusting Kick, Tsukami-uke, Yoko Kekomi

1

Start in back stance, kokutsu-dachi.

Side view.

2

Move your right hand up and "pick up" your left hand. This move combined with the next should be like drawing a curly "n' in the air with your right hand.

Side view.

3

Turn your right hand over into grasping block, tsukami-uke, and pull down.

4

Pull your right knee up between the arms.

Side view.

5

Kick down to lower level with side thrusting kick, yoko kekomi.

Side view.

157

Mountain Punch

Yama-zuki

Steps 34, 36, and 38 from **Bassai Dai** are referred to as mountain punches. They are so named because the shape of the body while doing the technique looks a bit like the Japanese kanji symbol for mountain, yama, rotated on its side.

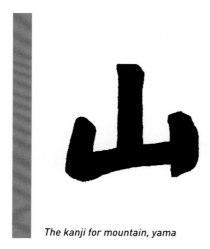

The kanji for mountain, yama

The mountain punch, yama-zuki

Correct Form

1 The upper arm is slightly inclined downward.

2 The punching hands are in line, as if against a wall.

3 The lower arm is slightly inclined upward.

4 Long narrow stance.

One-step Free Sparring

Jiyu Ippon Kumite

At the advanced level, the formal stances in sparring are dispensed with and so one-step free sparring is performed from a free fighting position. You should still continue the practice of bowing to your partner before and after sparring, and you must also announce each attack. You are free to move around before attacking, but do not get carried away and move without a purpose. The objective of your movement should be to improve your attack. When defending, you must also be light on your feet and should move and block as necessary to avoid being hit, while still being able to make a swift and effective counterattack.

HEAD LEVEL STEPPING PUNCH
Jodan Oi-zuki

1

Both opponents start in free fighting stance and the attacker announces "Jodan!"

2

The attacker steps and punches to the head, oi-zuki. The defender slides back and blocks with rising block, age-uke.

3

The defender punches with the reverse hand, gyaku-zuki. Hold this posture briefly before returning to fighting stance.

STOMACH LEVEL STEPPING PUNCH
Chudan Oi-zuki

1

Both opponents start in free fighting stance and the attacker announces "Chudan!"

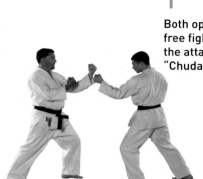

2

The attacker steps and punches to the stomach, oi-zuki. The defender slides back and blocks with outside block, soto-uke.

3

The defender punches with the reverse hand, gyaku-zuki. Hold this posture briefly before returning to fighting stance.

FRONT KICK

Mae-geri

A common mistake is to kick and then land too near to punch comfortably. Pushing the hips forward on the kick allows you to start a bit further away. As a result, you will be just the right distance away to do the punches.

1

Both opponents start in free fighting stance and the attacker announces "Mae-geri!"

2

The attacker executes a front kick, mae-geri, with the rear leg. The defender slides to the side and blocks with downward block, gedan barai.

3

The defender punches with the reverse hand, gyaku-zuki. Hold this posture briefly before returning to fighting stance.

SIDE THRUSTING KICK
Yoko Kekomi

1

Both opponents start in free-fighting stance and the attacker announces "Yoko kekomi!"

2

The attacker executes a side thrusting kick, yoko kekomi, with the rear leg. The defender slides to the side and blocks with outside block, soto-uke.

3

The defender punches with the reverse hand, gyaku-zuki. Hold this posture briefly before returning to fighting stance.

ROUNDHOUSE KICK
Mawashi-geri

1

Both opponents start in free-fighting stance and the attacker announces "Mawashi-geri!"

2

The attacker executes a roundhouse kick, mawashi-geri, with the rear leg. The defender slides back and blocks with inside block, uchi-uke.

3

The defender punches with the reverse hand, gyaku-zuki. Hold this posture briefly before returning to fighting stance.

BACK KICK
Ushiro-geri

1

Both opponents start in free-fighting stance and the attacker announces "Ushiro-geri!"

2

The attacker executes a back kick, ushiro-geri, with the rear leg. The defender slides to the side and blocks with outside block, soto-uke.

3

The defender punches with the reverse hand, gyaku-zuki. Hold this posture briefly before returning to fighting stance.

TRAINING TIPS

■ Try using different blocks. The ones shown are recommended, but you should feel free to find what works best for you. It is good to have a variety of defenses in your arsenal so that you do not become predictable, but remember that whatever you do has to actually work. When it comes to your grading examination, it is better to keep it simple than to try something difficult and get it wrong.

■ Beware of blocking with an open hand, particularly when defending against kicks. You are often better off getting kicked in the body than having a foot collide with your open fingers. Keeping a closed fist will protect your hands.

■ Kicks are powerful, so try to step out of the way rather than using brute force to block them. Front kick is particularly dangerous, and trying to directly parry it with your forearm could even result in a broken arm.

■ Be mindful of distancing and targeting. If you find that your attacks are falling short, you should increase your range. When kicking, this is done by pushing the hips farther forward toward the target. When punching, this can be done by sliding your front foot nearer to the target or by using a longer and deeper stance.

■ Control your anger. To attack and defend effectively you need to be strong and confident while keeping a focused mind. If you get angry, you will lose that focus.

CHAPTER **ELEVEN** kata application

The true meaning of karate is said to be contained within the kata. Kihon, the basic form, covers the building blocks from which the kata are formed. Kumite, the sparring forms, practice aspects like distancing and timing within a very constrained and artificial set of circumstances. However, if you wish to understand how karate operates as a real world fighting system, then you have to understand the karate kata. The way this is done in the karate dojo is through what is called bunkai or kata application.

Broadly, there are three types of bunkai.

Type 1 Surface Detail

These are sometimes called omote bunkai. They only look at the surface detail and take the moves in the kata at face value. If it looks like a block then it must be a block. Typically these applications are used to defend against classic karate attacks such as stepping punch or front kick and often are framed as part of a duel with the combatants starting the encounter out of arm's reach. There might be multiple attackers, and the application will deal with them in turn. The attackers will, of course, wait patiently until it is their turn to attack.

There are many advantages to this approach. These types of applications are simple to teach and learn. They match up well with the kata as traditionally practiced and so complement training in an obvious way. They are also very safe to practice with an opponent because they typically use punches, kicks, and blocks that don't really need to make any contact and leave out potentially dangerous techniques like joint locks and neck grabs.

The only disadvantage is that these kata applications are just not realistic fighting techniques; they tend to see all the techniques through the lens of modern karate, which revolves around a stand-up fight using punches and kicks. The result is that the real-life situations in which they can be used are limited, which is a real deal breaker for many karate practitioners who are understandably keen on the idea of learning a practical fighting art rather than an elaborate dance dressed up to look like a martial art.

Type 2 Secret Techniques

The second broad class of kata applications is sometimes referred to as ura bunkai, from the Japanese word meaning "behind." These applications look at the meaning hidden behind the surface detail. Blocks can be reinterpreted as joint locks, grappling holds, or strikes. The leg movements aren't just used to step or turn but can trip an opponent. The applications are usually framed in realistic self-defense scenarios, for example, defending against a swinging punch or starting in close with the attacker attempting to grab.

The obvious advantage of this approach is that ura bunkai produce realistic fighting techniques that can be used for self-defense in real life situations.

The ura bunkai are meant to be effective. But this can actually lead to one of its main disadvantages. The moves can in fact be just too dangerous to practice in any sort of realistic manner. For example, some bunkai include moves that grab the head and twist. When doing this sort of move with a training partner, you can go through the motions with a light touch and/or at slow speed. But any sort of realistic use of this move is clearly out of the question.

Another problem with the ura bunkai is that they often don't seem to match up very closely with the moves in the original kata. This makes it difficult for students to follow applications, no matter how well they know the moves of the kata. This is a shame because the whole premise of the kata is that they teach you fighting combinations; however, with ura bunkai there is a whole new step that has to be learned before you can actually make use of the moves. Even when this is overcome, for the purist it is still an unsatisfactory situation. And this leads to the third type of bunkai and the search for the ideal kata application.

Type 3 True Meaning

The third type of kata application has the effectiveness of the ura bunkai while remaining faithful to the original kata. This might even be the "one true meaning" of the kata moves, as envisioned by the original creator. Unfortunately, the intentions of the originators of the kata have long been lost in part due to successive karate masters teaching only omote bunkai. Also, given that the form of the kata has drifted somewhat over the years, trying to recover the original intent is a virtual impossibility. Nonetheless, the goal of finding the ideal bunkai for the kata is a worthy one.

Joint Locks

Grappling moves such as joint locks are largely ignored in karate classes. The kata, however, only really make sense if many of the moves that are labeled as blocks are actually interpreted as joint locks. Since the average karate grading syllabus completely ignores joint locks, the only place that the karate student will be exposed to them is when practicing kata application. Some karate practitioners will cross train in a grappling art such as jujutsu, judo, or aikido in order to get a better understanding of joint locks.

These joint locks work by hyperextending a joint such as the elbow, wrist, or shoulder. Take care when practising this with your partner. If an arm lock is being performed on you, make sure you communicate with your partner about when the arm lock is "on." A common convention is to "tap out," that is to indicate that you submit by tapping the floor or your opponent. When applying a joint lock, apply the technique slowly, allowing your partner to tap out if it is working. You need to work with your partner. If you get the technique wrong then the joint lock won't work at all, and your partner can give you feedback about that as well.

Trips and Throws

Trips and throws, often referred to as takedowns, is another set of techniques that are largely overlooked in karate practice. Many of the moves in the karate kata are moves that can be interpreted as throws. A big problem is that throwing someone who doesn't know how to land properly is dangerous. In the grappling arts such as judo, one of the first things students are taught is how to land safely, a technique called breakfalling, because without this foundation it isn't possible to practice throwing techniques in class. Another precaution is to use rubberized mats to help break the fall. This is standard practice in the judo dojo but less common in the karate class.

If your partner has not been taught how to breakfall, or you do not have a safe surface to fall on, then you should avoid performing throws. Under these circumstances you can still practice kata applications that include throws by working up to the point where you need to throw. At that point, just get the feeling that you could unbalance or lift your opponent, but without actually going through with it. With some moves it is possible to support your partner's weight as he goes down, effectively placing him on the floor as a simulation for the takedown technique.

Examples

Some of these kata applications can be dangerous. If you practice these applications with a partner, it should be done with extreme care so as to ensure that you do not cause an injury. For this reason, it is highly recommended that you practice kata applications at slow speed.

STEPPING THROUGH THROWDOWN (KIHON KATA)

Simplistic interpretations of Kihon Kata typically show the first move defending against a stepping punch from the side. This is usually demonstrated with the attacker being so far away that if the defender didn't move, it wouldn't even reach him. The example application shown here tries to address that by using the preparation for the downward block as the actual defense.

1

The attacker starts in front stance with the left leg forward. The attacker steps and punches with his right hand. Deflect the punch with your left hand while simultaneously attacking with a low punch using your right hand.

2

Step alongside and attack the groin with your left fist.

3

Step past the attacker with your right foot and use your right arm and hip to throw your opponent.

HAMMER ESCAPE (HEIAN SHODAN)

This is a simple application of the hammer fist strike (step 4) in Heian Shodan. This works well as an exercise for practicing this move and helps you get used to the idea that you need to coordinate your body movement with the arm action in order to maximize power. By working this drill through with your partner you will discover the limitations of this kind of escape. If your opponent manages to get a firm grip, then you will find it difficult to escape. You can mitigate this by learning to react quickly. As soon as they go for the grab, pull back vigorously, and you will be able to escape before they tighten their grip.

1

The attacker grabs your wrist.

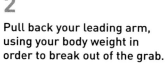

2

Pull back your leading arm, using your body weight in order to break out of the grab.

3

Continue moving your hand round in an arc and target the clavicle (collarbone) using a hammer fist strike.

DEADLY TURN (HEIAN SHODAN)

A more advanced application uses the turn at the beginning of the kata to throw an opponent. The footwork is slightly different from the kata but uses the same angles. This application is presented here to illustrate a more realistic application but should be performed with caution.

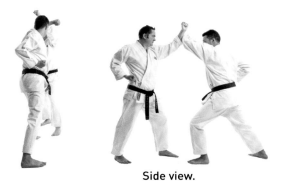

Side view.

1

Attacker brings his arm down in a stabbing attack. Block with left side rising block.

Side view.

2

Grab the attacker's wrist, and step out to the right and turn to the side. At the same time, use the downward block arm motion to pull the attacker's arm out to the side (Heian Shodan step 1).

Side view.

3

Step forward and hit with stepping punch, oi-zuki (Heian Shodan step 2).

4

Reach around your opponent's neck and grab his chin.

Side view.

5

Step backwards and use the downward block motion to throw your opponent (Heian Shodan step 3). WARNING: This is a very dangerous technique and should only be practiced at slow motion and with the full cooperation of your sparring partner.

Side view.

6

Defender uses downward hammer fist strike, tetsui-uchi (Heian Shodan step 4).

Side view.

ARM TRAP COUNTER STRIKE (HEIAN NIDAN)

This is a simple omote-style application of steps 1, 2, and 3 in Heian Nidan that will help in developing these techniques.

1

The attacker prepares to attack with a hook punch.

2

Block using head level inside block, jodan uchi-uke (Heian Nidan step 1).

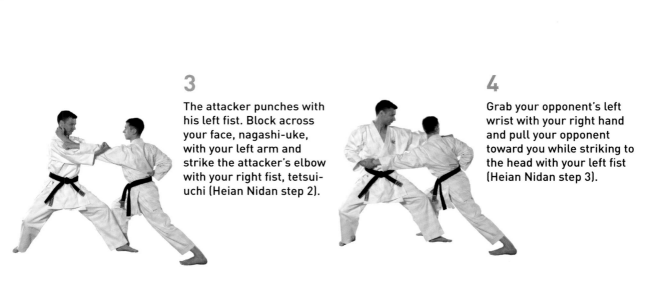

3

The attacker punches with his left fist. Block across your face, nagashi-uke, with your left arm and strike the attacker's elbow with your right fist, tetsui-uchi (Heian Nidan step 2).

4

Grab your opponent's left wrist with your right hand and pull your opponent toward you while striking to the head with your left fist (Heian Nidan step 3).

HIP KICK BREAKTHROUGH (HEIAN NIDAN)

Moves 17 and 20 from Heian Nidan are usually referred to as inside blocks. This can lead people to try to use them to deflect attacks, but there is a problem here. In general, you should block using your front hand. The blocks as they appear in the kata are not effective for this because they use the rear hand. The application shown here uses the preparation part of the motion, the so-called "cup-and-saucer" position where the fists move to the hip, to disrupt a grabbing hand. The final part of the movement is used to deliver a backfist strike. The front kick is then used to further weaken the opponent's stance by targeting his hip. When you practice this move with a partner, you should perform this as more of a push than a hit so as to avoid injury while still retaining the feeling of using the attack to knock the hip back, turning your opponent.

1

Your opponent grips your left upper arm with his right hand.

2

Pull down on your opponent's right wrist with your left hand and at the same time smash down on his forearm near the middle of his arm with your right (Heian Nidan step 17).

3

Using your right fist, hit the side of your opponent's neck with a backfist strike (Heian Nidan step 17).

4

Front kick with your right leg, pushing through your opponent's left hip (Heian Nidan step 18).

5

Follow up with a reverse punch using your left fist (Heian Nidan step 19).

TURNING ELBOW DEFENSE (HEIAN SANDAN)

This is a simple exercise using moves 14 and 15 in Heian Sandan that will help in developing these techniques. You will notice that if the backfist strike does not follow the correct path, the opponent's arm will obstruct it.

1

The attacker prepares to attack with a stepping punch.

2

As the attacker punches, step back and block using your left elbow.

3

Hit with a backfist strike, uraken-uchi, to the head, moving your arm in a vertical plane to bypass your opponent's arm.

SPINNING WRIST ESCAPE (HEIAN SANDAN)

This application uses step 9 from Heian Sandan to deal with a wrist grab. One of the advantages of this technique is that it assumes that it is impossible to break the grip. Instead, it fl ws around the grab and counterstrikes from an unexpected angle.

1

The attacker grabs your right wrist.

2

Turn away, leaving the trapped arm in place.

3

Continue turning, bending your trapped arm behind your back. Step through with your left leg and strike with your left arm.

ARM TRAP TAKEDOWN (HEIAN SANDAN)

The first six moves from Heian Sandan are often described as blocks, and this has led to unrealistic omote bunkai interpretations for these moves, repeatedly blocking an opponent's attacks but then offering no counterattack. The double-handed move is sometimes even explained as a defense against two simultaneous punches. A more realistic interpretation of the simultaneous inside and downward blocks from Heian Sandan is as an arm lock. This technique works by hyperextending the elbow joint, so remember to take the usual precautions when performing this technique.

1

The attacker reaches for a grab with his right hand. Step out to the left side by moving your right foot round behind you and deflect your opponent's arm to the side.

2

Grab your opponent's wrist with your right hand and twist it so that his hand is palm up. Pull his arm straight and bring your left arm under his left elbow using the inside block motion (Heian Sandan step 1).

3

Lift your opponent's wrist with your right hand and drop your left hand.

4

Attack the joint again by dropping your right hand and striking up with your left against your opponent's elbow (Heian Sandan steps 2 and 3).

5

Your opponent will tend to react by lifting his arm and shoulder. Continue the flow of this motion by pushing his arm up over your shoulder to your left (Heian Sandan step 7).

6

Continue moving your opponent's arm so that it comes around behind you. Wrap your left arm around his right arm and trap it with a position much like pressing block (Heian Sandan step 8).

7

Step forward with your right foot so that you come alongside your opponent's right hip (Heian Sandan step 9).

Side view.

8

Bring your left leg round behind you and push with your right hand so that you throw your opponent to the ground (Heian Sandan step 10).

WRIST GRAB REVERSAL (HEIAN YONDAN)

The classic omote applications for moves 5 to 7 in Heian Yondan are performed at quite long range and use the backfist strikes to block a stepping punch. The preparatory hand positions are just that, preparations for the backfist and elbow strike, and serve no other purpose.

The application shown here uses the action where the fists are brought to the hip, the so-called "cup-and-saucer position," to break a grip and apply a wrist lock.

1

The attacker grabs your clothing with his right hand.

2

Reach over with your right hand and grip on top of the attacker's hand while your left hand grabs from underneath.

3

Use both hands to break the grip and twist, bringing them to your right hip. Use your left elbow to help push and straighten your opponent's arm by pushing on his right elbow (Heian Yondan step 5).

4

Grab your opponent's head (Heian Yondan step 6).

5

Kick the back of your opponent's leg with your left leg and simultaneously pull back his head with your left hand.

6

Place your left hand behind your opponent's head and strike with your right elbow (Heian Yondan step 7).

RAPID COUNTERSTRIKE (HEIAN YONDAN)

There are many possible applications of moves 11 and 12 in Heian Yondan. These moves consist of simultaneous blocks and strikes followed by a kick and a close-range finishing move. One possible application that will help in developing these techniques is shown here. This application has its drawbacks: the preparation hand in the first step is really not doing anything useful, and the block in the second step is quite awkward and needs accurate timing to get right. Nonetheless, this application serves as a solid omote drill for practicing the techniques.

1

The attacker punches to stomach level with a right-hand stepping punch. Step into front stance at an angle away from the attack, while blocking with your left hand and preparing with your right hand (Heian Yondan step 11a).

2

The attacker follows up with a left punch to head level. Deflect the punch with your left hand and if possible try to grab your opponent's wrist as you do this. At the same time, strike to head level with a knife-hand strike, shuto-uchi (Heian Yondan step 11b).

3

Kick to the groin or stomach with front kick, mae-geri (Heian Yondan step 12a).

4

In a real-life situation, the stomach kick would tend to make your opponent bend forward. Enhance this motion by pulling with your left hand. Finish with a downward elbow strike, empi-uchi, to the back of the neck (Heian Yondan step12c).

If you find that your opponent manages to remain upright after step 3, then, as an alternative, finish with a back-hand strike, uraken-uchi, to the nose or whatever target you find available.

CLOSE RANGE RAPID COUNTERSTRIKE (HEIAN YONDAN)

An alternative application for steps 11 and 12 in Heian Yondan starts with a much closer range situation where your opponent is using both arms to grab. It overcomes some of the shortcomings of the previous application, using every single arm movement from the kata to do something.

1

Your opponent goes to grab with both hands.

2

Bring your left hand over the top of your opponent's right arm. At the same time, bring your right hand up through the center against your opponent's left arm.

3

Sweep your opponent's right hand out to the left and his left hand out to the right.

4

Bring your left hand over to the right and make contact with the outside edge of your opponent's left arm.

5

Sweep your opponent's left arm over to your left, trying to grab his wrist in the process. This makes the way clear to hit to the temple with a right knife-hand strike.

6

Use front kick with your right leg against whatever target is available (Heian Yondan step 12a).

7

If you did manage to grab the wrist then you can apply an arm bar by pulling your opponent's left arm straight and pushing on the elbow with your right elbow. Otherwise, you have the option of hitting with a backfist strike.

WEDGE-BLOCK ESCAPE (HEIAN YONDAN)

Moves 13–16 can be applied to defend against a throttling attack. Alternatively, your opponent could grab your lapels, potentially as a prelude to a head butt.

1

The attacker uses both hands to grab some clothing or the throat.

2

Push your fists up in between your opponent's arms. This will act as an initial barrier to any potential head butt. Step backward into back stance and use wedge block, kakiwake-uke, to weaken the grip and pull the attacker forward (Heian Yondan step 13).

3

Counterattack by using a knee strike or, if there is space, a kick (Heian Yondan step 14).

4

Continue the counter-attack with head level punches (Heian Yondan step 15 and 16).

STANDING ARM BAR (HEIAN GODAN)

Move 10 in Heian Godan has open hands twisting together and then finishing one on top of the other in front of the hip. The standard interpretation is as an arm bar with one hand twisting the opponent's wrist while the other presses on the elbow. The move is not used in isolation—as is common in karate, the joint lock is used as a way of setting up some striking techniques.

1

Your opponent grabs your left wrist.

2

Place your right fist under your left wrist (Heian Godan step 8 but note that the arms are reversed, right arm under left).

3

Initially, pull your trapped hand back but then quickly change direction and push up, using your right hand to assist (Heian Godan step 9).

4

Twist your left hand and try to grip your opponent's wrist. At the same time, bring your left hand onto your opponent's right elbow.

5

Pull your opponent's arm down and to the right, pulling on the wrist with your right hand and pushing on the elbow with your left (Heian Godan step 10).

6

Keeping hold of your opponent's wrist with your right hand, hit with your left hand using a hammer fist strike (Heian Godan step 11).

7

Step with your right foot and punch with your right hand. This should be targeted at the side of your opponent's head (Heian Godan step 12).

One of the strengths of this application is that it can deal with a variety of different attacks. The initial move is slightly different, but the follow-up actions are just the same. For example, if the attacker starts off with a hooking punch, block it with one hand then shoot up with the other to make the head level cross block position. From then on the application proceeds as before.

1

Your opponent attacks with hooking punch using his right hand. Block with your left hand.

2

Immediately bring your right hand up so that it touches the outside edge of your opponent's wrist.

3

Grab your opponent's wrist with your right hand while your left travels to his elbow. This is the same position as step 4 from the previous application and so you proceed with the same follow up: arm bar, hammer fist strike, punch.

The classic attack that the cross-block is used against is an overhead stabbing attack. Usually it doesn't make sense to use up both hands dealing with an attack. In most cases you would want to use your second arm to counterstrike, ideally simultaneously with the block, or leave it free to deal with the next attack. In this case, however, it could be a strong attack, possibly with a weapon, and so using both arms for added strength might be justified.

1

The attacker lifts his arm above his head ready to attack.

2

As the attacker swings down at your head, shoot both your hands up to intercept it using cross block. From here you can transition to the arm bar.

WHIRLWIND TAKEDOWN (HEIAN GODAN)

The crescent kick and elbow strike in Heian Godan are techniques that karate practitioners readily understand, kicking and striking an opponent. The reinforced block, the rising punch, and the jump that follow, however, often lead to some unrealistic and quite strange interpretations. The so-called rising punch, tsuki-age, causes a lot of confusion because although it looks like a punch, it is performed while facing the other way. You might see this sort of thing in the movies but never in a boxing or mixed martial arts match. The jump has quite often been interpreted as a defense against an opponent with a long stick swinging at your legs, but this doesn't seem like a likely way to attack with a stick and I have yet to see a demonstration of this that made any sense of this.

The application presented here twists and turns, defending against an opponent from behind. It uses rotation to unbalance, attack, and then throw the opponent. It starts with steps 14, 15, and 16 in Heian Godan. The first of these techniques is usually referred to as a block, but it is performed slowly in the kata, suggesting a locking or breaking technique. This application then continues using steps 17 and 18 to lift your opponent. The jump is interpreted as being part of a throw. Steps 19 and 20 then apply an arm lock on the ground.

This is a lengthy application, taking in 7 moves from the kata, but this is how applications ideally should be. The initial attack is dealt with; then countering distracts and weakens the opponent's posture before taking him to the ground and finishing him off.

The application is shown starting with a grab from behind, but there are many other scenarios that could kick it off and yet still get the same result. The key is to have access to the opponent's center so that you can get in and perform the throw.

1

The attacker grabs your collar from behind.

2

Turn, dragging your fingers across the attacker's face and try to catch the attacker's arm under your armpit (Heian Godan step 14).

3

Grab your opponent and strike his leg with a crescent kick (Heian Godan step 15).

4

Immediately follow through with an elbow strike to your opponent's head (Heian Godan step 16).

5

Slide in close to your opponent, pushing your right shoulder into his chest and reaching through under his arm with your right arm (Heian Godan step 17).

6

Rotate your body, bend your knees, and hoist your opponent up onto your back by pulling with your left arm and lifting with your right (Heian Godan step 18).

7

Step through with your right foot and throw your opponent over your shoulder (Heian Godan step 19a).

8

Retain a hold on your opponent's right arm. Thread your left arm through under your opponent's elbow and then brace it by gripping your own right wrist. Make sure that your opponent's right forearm is trapped against the side of your body (Heian Godan step 19b).

9

Step through with your right foot and rotate to your left applying pressure to your opponent's shoulder joint (Heian Godan step 20). Make sure that you keep your back straight so that your opponent's arm is lifted up, or the lock won't work.

SINGLE ARM TAKEDOWN (HEIAN GODAN)

The swastika block, manji-uke, is often described as a simultaneous downward block and head level inside block. There is, however, no credible explanation for why someone would do two blocks at the same time, especially in opposite directions. More realistically, one hand is doing a pulling action while the other strikes or unbalances the opponent. The simplest version of this deals with a front kick by sidestepping and using the preparation position for manji-uke to deflect the kick to the side. It then uses one arm to yank the leg up while the other arm assists by pushing the opponent over.

1

Both you and your opponent start in fighting stance with left leg forward.

2

Your opponent kicks with his right leg. Sidestep by pivoting on your left foot and deflect the kick to your right by sweeping across with your right arm.

3

Hook your right arm under your opponent's kick leg and swing round with your left arm and push on your opponent's chest.

4

Tip your opponent over by lifting with your right arm and pushing down with your left.

In Heian Godan, the swastika block is combined with another motion that changes the way the application works slightly and allows it to work as a follow-up to a head punch. This simple application of moves 21 and 22 in Heian Godan uses the preparation as a defense while simultaneously reaching in and grabbing. It is immediately followed by the swastika block, which performs the takedown as before, with one arm pulling the opponent's supporting leg and the other pushing so that they are tipped up.

1

The attacker starts with the right leg forward. Face your opponent in natural stance.

2

The attacker punches to head level with a left-hand stepping punch. Step forward into front stance and block across the face with your left hand, while striking down to your opponent's leg with your right hand (Heian Godan step 21).

3

Strike down with your left fist while simultaneously pulling with your right, thus unbalancing your opponent (Heian Godan step 22).

RETURNING WAVE TAKEDOWN (TEKKI SHODAN)

Karate training typically focuses on fighting at a distance, throwing long range attacks to reach an opponent before they can reach you. In reality, fights often end up at close range with an opponent grabbing you. Tekki Shodan contains various tactics for dealing with this situation.

This is a simple application of steps 23 to 26 in Tekki Shodan and uses side-to-side motions to break a hold. It uses the returning wave kicks to help to break an opponent's stance. Note that both kicks attack the same knee.

1

The attacker grabs you with both hands.

2

Grab the attacker and use a returning wave kick with your right foot to attack your opponent's right knee (Tekki Shodan step 24a).

3

Pull your opponent to the right using both hands (Tekki Shodan step 24b).

4

Use a left-foot returning wave kick to attack the right knee (Tekki Shodan step 26a).

5

Pull the attacker to the left using both hands (Tekki Shodan step 26b).

CLINCH BREAKER (TEKKI SHODAN)

This application is used to deal with a grappling clinch hold called a double collar tie, which controls an opponent from the front by using both hands to grab behind the neck.

1

Start in a clinch with your opponent holding you with his hands over your neck.

2

Reach in underneath your opponent's arms and grab around his neck.

3

Bring your left arm over the top of your opponent's right arm, breaking his hold.

4

Drag your opponent's right arm back toward your hip and trap it against your body (Tekki Shodan step 2).

5

With your right hand behind your opponent's head, strike with your left elbow, empi-uchi (Tekki Shodan step 3).

CLINCH DOMINATION STRIKE (TEKKI SHODAN)

In the case where an opponent's clinch hold is too tight to get inside, an alternative tactic needs to be employed. This application uses the hand movements in Tekki Shodan as strikes.

1
Start in a clinch with your opponent holding you with his hands over your neck.

2
Press down on your opponent's arms with your right forearm and use your left arm in the backfist strike to press against the left hand side of your opponent's head (Tekki Shodan step 9).

3
Pull your left arm back ready to strike.

4
Swing back, striking the left side of your opponent's neck with your forearm. As you do this motion, rotate your forearm so that you hit with the bony edge (Tekki Shodan step 11).

5
Repeat, using returning wave kicks to distract your opponent (Tekki Shodan steps 11 and 13).

6
If your opponent tries moving his head out of range, straighten your arm and switch to hitting with hammer fist strike (Tekki Shodan step 14).

189

FRONT GRAB ESCAPE (BASSAI DAI)

There are many explanations for the very first move in Bassai Dai. Some omote bunkai treat it as a block, but this is problematic because the forward movement means that the distancing doesn't work out. Either it is too close for the block to be practical or it is too far away for the opponent to have realistically been able to attack. More realistic approaches use the entire movement as a wrist lock, and this does work much better. The application shown here uses the initial part of the movement, where the hands move back to the left hip, as a way of breaking a grab. The second part of the move is treated as a backfist strike.

1

The attacker grabs from the front. This could be directed at your neck in a throttling action or it could be grasping hold of your lapels as a prelude to a head butt.

2

Bring your hands inside the grab with your left forearm vertical against your opponent's right forearm near to his elbow.

3

Break your opponent's grip by pushing against the inside of your opponent's right arm with your left. Support this movement with your right hand by pushing against your left wrist. When you do this, your left arm should roll over your opponent's arm and grab above the elbow.

4

Continue moving your left arm so that it wraps around your opponent's right arm, trapping it. Push your left hand up toward your opponent's chin, applying pressure to the upper part of his arm.

5

Push your weight forward and attack with a backfist strike using your right hand.

WRIST LOCK (BASSAI DAI)

This application uses moves 17 to 19 in Bassai Dai. It uses the grasping lock to apply a wrist lock. The purpose of this is just to turn your opponent's body slightly, enough to weaken his stance so that you can attack with a side thrusting kick. Usually this kick is practiced to stomach level, but in this application we have a more realistic height, attacking the knees. Note that in order to get a powerful attack it is still necessary to lift your knee quite high, allowing you to drop your weight down on the target and making for a very powerful attack.

1

The attacker punches with the right hand. Step back and use a knife-hand block to deflect the attack (Bassai Dai step 17).

2

Grab your opponent's hand with your left hand. Use grasping block, tsukami-uke, to apply a wrist lock (Bassai Dai step 18).

3

Lift your knee and use side thrusting kick to attack the knee (Bassai Dai move 19). IMPORTANT: When practicing this move with a partner, you must perform this kick in slow motion and your opponent should flow with the attack, turning his body and bending his knee away from the kick to avoid injury.

ELBOW STRIKE ENTRAPMENT (BASSAI DAI)

Moves 31, 32, and 33 from Bassai Dai are sometimes described as reinforced downward blocks, and sometimes as punches. The omote explanations for these moves are unconvincing and have difficulty explaining why you would be punching or blocking in horse riding stance, legs spread facing an opponent. This application uses the previous move, step 30 in Bassai Dai, an elbow strike, to apply a wrist lock that drags an opponent's head down into a barrage of hammer hand strikes.

1

The attacker grabs your right wrist with his left hand.

2

Lift your right elbow, rolling it over your opponent's hand so that it starts to apply pressure to his wrist.

3

Place your left hand on your opponent's hand, trapping it. Push your elbow down while turning your body and drop your weight into horse riding stance. This needs to apply a wrist lock that causes your opponent's head to drop down in front of you (Bassai Dai step 30).

4

Grab your opponent's wrist with your left hand and use your right hand to hit with a hammer fist strike to your opponent's head.

5

Pull your right fist back, ready for another strike while at the same time dragging your opponent in by pulling back with your left hand.

6

Hammer fist strike again with your right hand.

MOUNTAIN PUNCH MANEUVER (BASSAI DAI)

This application uses moves 35, 36, and 37 from Bassai Dai. The omote approach would interpret this as two simultaneous punches, one to the face and one to the body or groin. A more satisfying approach is to treat only one of the arm movements as a punch while the other acts as a block or, as in the case of the bunkai presented here, as a way of twisting out of a grab.

1

Attacker grabs your left arm with his left with the intention of following up with a punch.

2

Pull your left arm back slightly then abruptly reverse the direction pushing it out to your left and turning your fist over your opponent's hand so that your knuckles face down. Lift your right fist to head height, slide your left foot forward, and lean in enough to hit with the mountain punch.

3

Grab your opponent's right wrist with your left hand. Slide your weight back, bringing your left foot back to meet your right while dragging your opponent's arm. As you do this, apply an arm bar by pushing your right fist on his elbow.

APPENDICES

Grading Syllabus

WHITE BELT GRADING SYLLABUS	
Basics	
Stepping punch	Oi-zuki
Rising block	Age-uke
Outside block	Soto-uke
Inside block	Uchi-uke
Front kick	Mae-geri
Kata	
Kihon Kata (Taikyoku Shodan)	
Kumite	
Five-step sparring	Gohon kumite

ORANGE BELT GRADING SYLLABUS	
Basics	
Stepping punch	Oi-zuki
Rising block	Age-uke
Outside block	Soto-uke
Inside block	Uchi-uke
Knife-hand block	Shuto-uke
Front kick	Mae-geri
Side thrusting kick	Yoko kekomi
Side rising kick	Yoko keage
Kata	
Kihon Kata (Taikyoku Shodan)	
Heian Shodan	
Kumite	
Five-step sparring	Gohon kumite

RED BELT GRADING SYLLABUS

Basics

Triple punch	Sanbon tsuki
Rising block, reverse punch	Age-uke, gyaku-zuki
Outside block, reverse punch	Soto-uke, gyaku-zuki
Inside block, reverse punch	Uchi-uke, gyaku-zuki
Knife-hand block	Shuto-uke
Front kick	Mae-geri
Side thrusting kick	Yoko kekomi
Side rising kick	Yoko keage

Kata

Kihon Kata (Taikyoku Shodan)

Heian Shodan

Heian Nidan

Kumite

Five-step sparring	Gohon kumite

YELLOW BELT GRADING SYLLABUS

Basics

Triple punch	Sanbon tsuki
Rising block, reverse punch, downward block	Age-uke, gyaku-zuki, gedan barai
Outside block, elbow strike	Soto-uke, empi-uchi
Inside block, reverse punch	Uchi-uke, gyaku-zuki
Knife-hand block, spear-hand strike	Shuto-uke, nukite-uchi
Consecutive front kicks	Mae ren-geri
Side thrusting kick	Yoko kekomi
Side rising kick	Yoko keage

Kata

Kihon Kata (Taikyoku Shodan)

Heian Shodan

Heian Nidan

Heian Sandan

Kumite

One-step sparring	Ippon kumite
Head level stepping punch	Jodan oi-zuki
Stomach level stepping punch	Chudan oi-zuki

GREEN BELT GRADING SYLLABUS

Basics

Triple punch	Sanbon tsuki
Rising block, reverse punch, downward block	Age-uke, gyaku-zuki, gedan barai
Outside block, elbow strike, backfist strike	Soto-uke, empi-uchi, uraken-uchi
Inside block, jabbing punch, reverse punch	Uchi-uke, kizami-zuki, gyaku-zuki
Knife-hand block, jabbing front kick, spear-hand strike	Shuto-uke, kizami mae-geri, nukite-uchi
Consecutive front kicks	Mae ren-geri
Side thrusting kick	Yoko kekomi
Side rising kick	Yoko keage
Roundhouse kick	Mawashi-geri

Kata

Kihon Kata (Taikyoku Shodan)

Heian Shodan

Heian Nidan

Heian Sandan

Heian Yondan

Kumite

One-step sparring	Ippon kumite
Head level stepping punch	Jodan oi-zuki
Stomach level stepping punch	Chudan oi-zuki
Front kick	Mae-geri
Side thrusting kick	Yoko kekomi

PURPLE BELT GRADING SYLLABUS

Basics

Triple punch	Sanbon tsuki
Rising block, reverse punch, downward block	Age-uke, gyaku-zuki, gedan barai
Outside block, elbow strike, backfist strike, reverse punch	Soto-uke, empi-uchi, uraken-uchi, gyaku-zuki
Inside block, jabbing punch, reverse punch	Uchi-uke, kizami-zuki, gyaku-zuki
Knife-hand block, jabbing front kick, spear-hand strike	Shuto-uke, kizami mae-geri, nukite-uchi
Consecutive front kicks	Mae ren-geri
Side thrusting kick	Yoko kekomi
Side rising kick	Yoko keage
Roundhouse kick	Mawashi-geri

Kata

Kihon Kata (Taikyoku Shodan)

Heian Shodan

Heian Nidan

Heian Sandan

Heian Yondan

Heian Godan

Kumite

One-step sparring	Ippon kumite
Head level stepping punch	Jodan oi-zuki
Stomach level stepping punch	Chudan oi-zuki
Front kick	Mae-geri
Side thrusting kick	Yoko kekomi

PURPLE AND WHITE BELT GRADING SYLLABUS

Basics

Triple punch	Sanbon tsuki
Rising block, reverse punch, downward block	Age-uke, gyaku-zuki, gedan barai
Outside block, elbow strike, backfist strike, reverse punch, downward block	Soto-uke, empi-uchi, uraken-uchi, gyaku-zuki, gedan barai
Inside block, jabbing punch, reverse punch, downward block	Uchi-uke, kizami-zuki, gyaku-zuki, gedan barai
Knife-hand block, jabbing front kick, spear-hand strike	Shuto-uke, kizami mae-geri, nukite-uchi
Consecutive front kicks	Mae ren-geri
Side thrusting kick	Yoko kekomi
Side rising kick	Yoko keage
Roundhouse kick	Mawashi-geri
Back kick	Ushiro-geri

Kata

Kihon Kata (Taikyoku Shodan)

Heian Shodan

Heian Nidan

Heian Sandan

Heian Yondan

Heian Godan

Tekki Shodan

Kumite

One-step sparring	Ippon kumite
Head level stepping punch	Jodan oi-zuki
Stomach level stepping punch	Chudan oi-zuki
Front kick	Mae-geri
Side thrusting kick	Yoko kekomi
Roundhouse kick	Mawashi-geri

BROWN BELT GRADING SYLLABUS

Basics

Triple punch	Kizami-zuki, oi-zuki, gyaku-zuki
Front kick combination	Mae-geri, oi-zuki, gyaku-zuki
Side thrusting kick combination	Yoko kekomi, uraken-uchi, gyaku-zuki
Roundhouse kick combination	Mawashi-geri, uraken-uchi, gyaku-zuki
Back kick combination	Ushiro-geri, uraken-uchi, gyaku-zuki

Kata

Kihon Kata (Taikyoku Shodan)

Heian Shodan

Heian Nidan

Heian Sandan

Heian Yondan

Heian Godan

Tekki Shodan

Bassai Dai

Kumite

One-step free sparring	Jiyu ippon kumite
Head level stepping punch	Jodan oi-zuki
Stomach level stepping punch	Chudan oi-zuki
Front kick	Mae-geri
Side thrusting kick	Yoko kekomi
Roundhouse kick	Mawashi-geri
Back kick	Ushiro-geri

BLACK BELT GRADING SYLLABUS

Basics

Triple punch	Kizami-zuki, oi-zuki, gyaku-zuki
Front kick combination	Mae-geri, oi-zuki, gyaku-zuki
Side thrusting kick combination	Yoko kekomi, uraken-uchi, gyaku-zuki
Roundhouse kick combination	Mawashi-geri, uraken-uchi, gyaku-zuki
Back kick combination	Ushiro-geri, uraken-uchi, gyaku-zuki
Four-kick combination	Mae-geri, yoko kekomi, mawashi-geri, ushiro-geri, uraken-uchi, gyaku-zuki
Standing kicks	Mae-geri, yoko kekomi, ushiro-geri
Black Belt combination	

Kata

Kihon Kata (Taikyoku Shodan)

Heian Shodan

Heian Nidan

Heian Sandan

Heian Yondan

Heian Godan

Tekki Shodan

Choose one from:

Bassai Dai, Kanku Dai, Jion, Empi, Hangetsu

Kumite

One-step free sparring	Jiyu ippon kumite
Head level stepping punch	Jodan oi-zuki
Stomach level stepping punch	Chudan oi-zuki
Front kick	Mae-geri
Side thrusting kick	Yoko kekomi
Roundhouse kick	Mawashi-geri
Back kick	Ushiro-geri
Free sparring	Jiyu-kumite

Shotokan Karate Kata

太極初段 KIHON KATA (TAIKYOKU SHODAN)

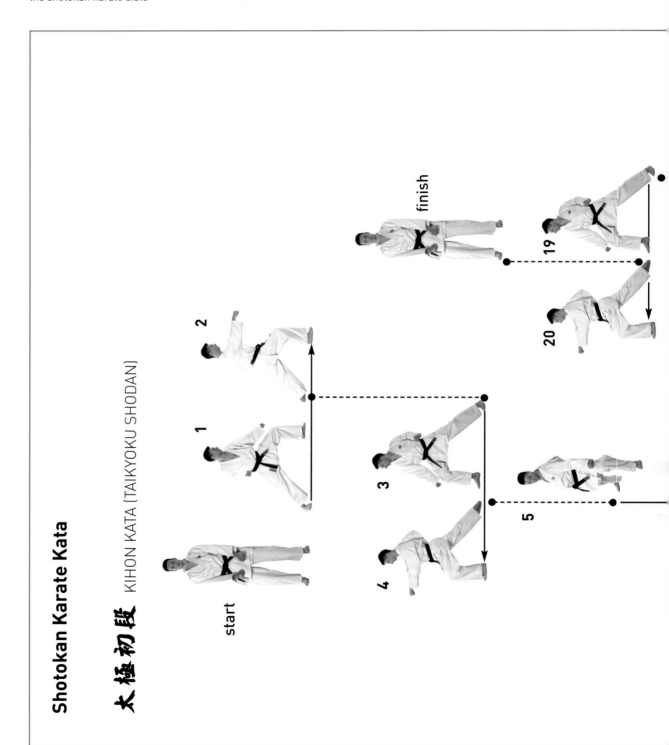

start

finish

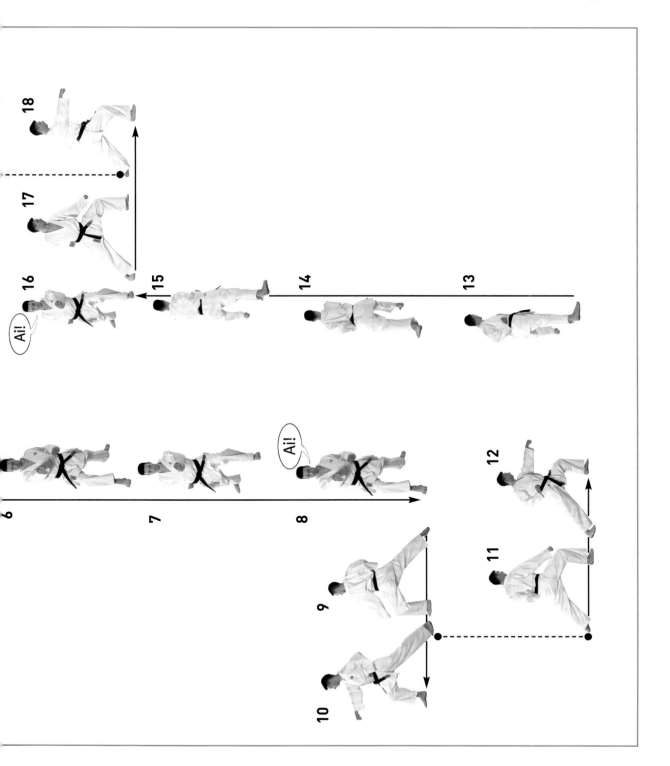

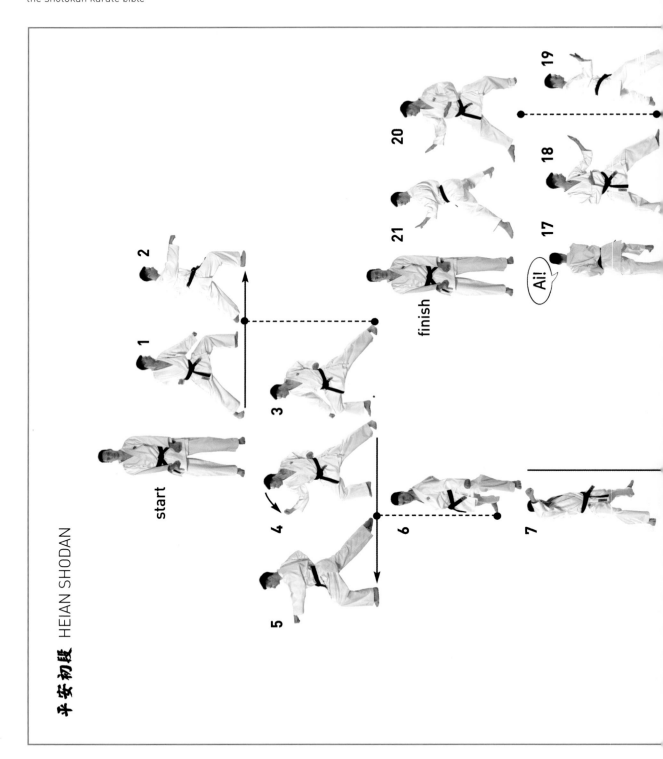

平安初段 HEIAN SHODAN

start

1

2

3

4

5

6

7

finish

17

18

19

20

21

Ai!

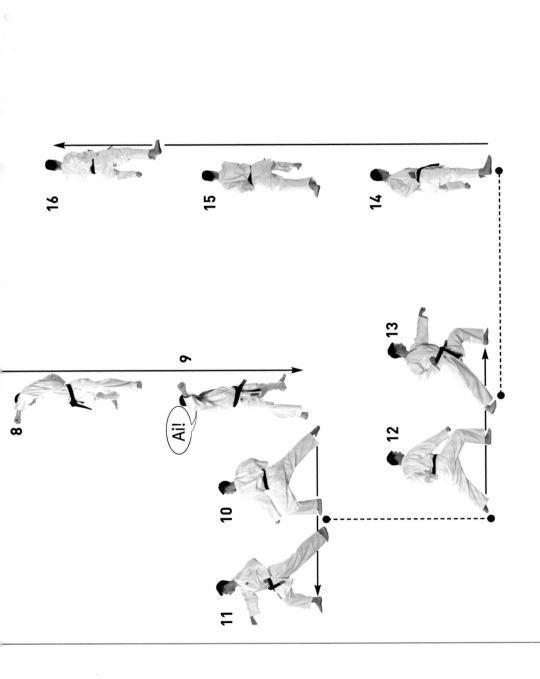

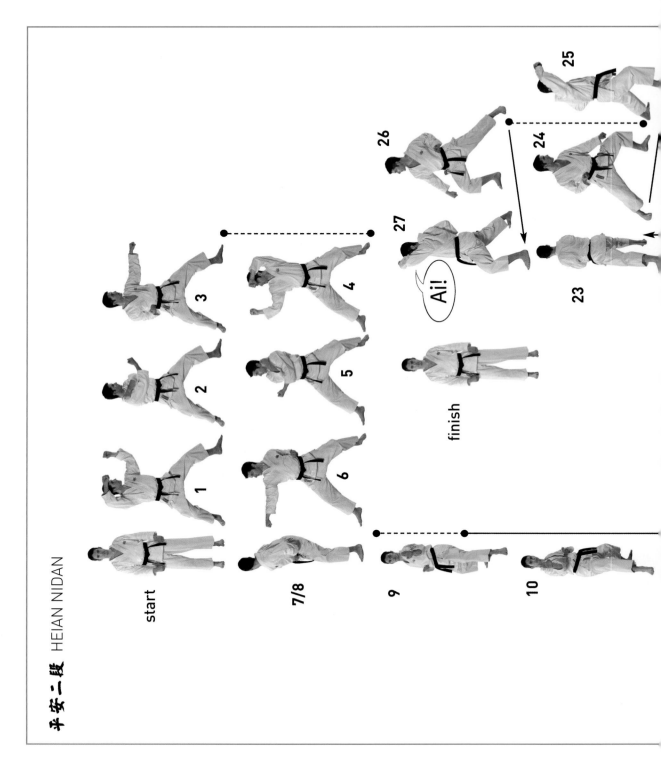

平安二段 HEIAN NIDAN

start

1 2 3

4 5 6

7/8 9 10

23 24 25 26 27

Ai!

finish

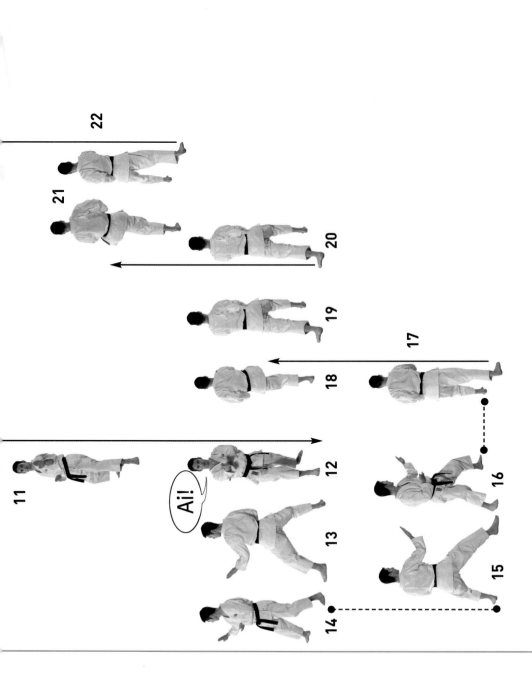

平安三段 HEIAN SANDAN

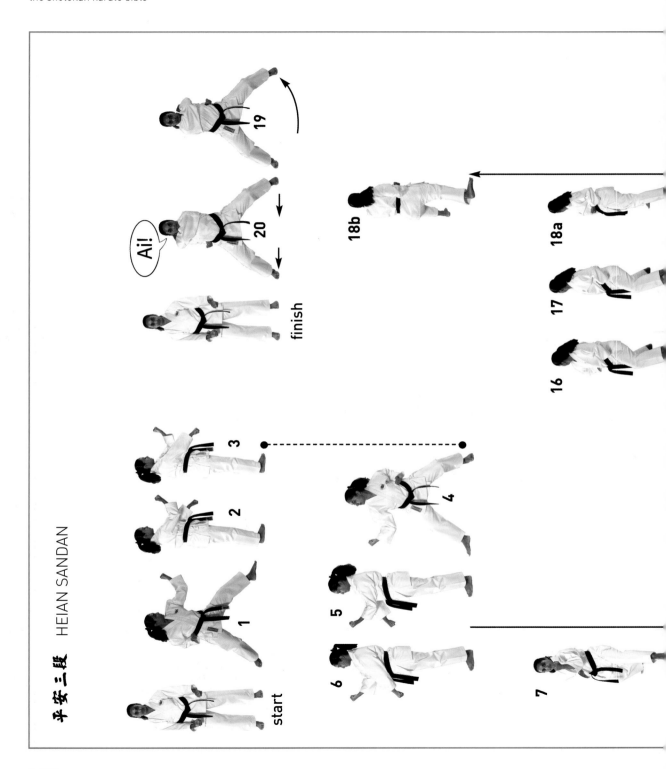

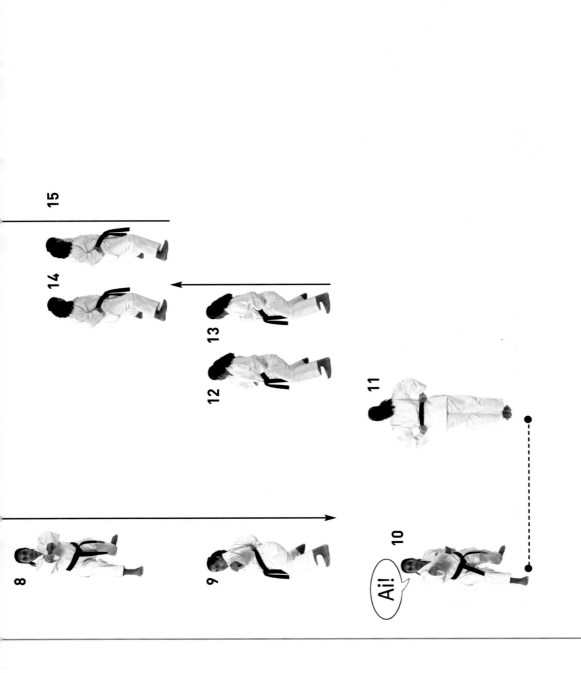

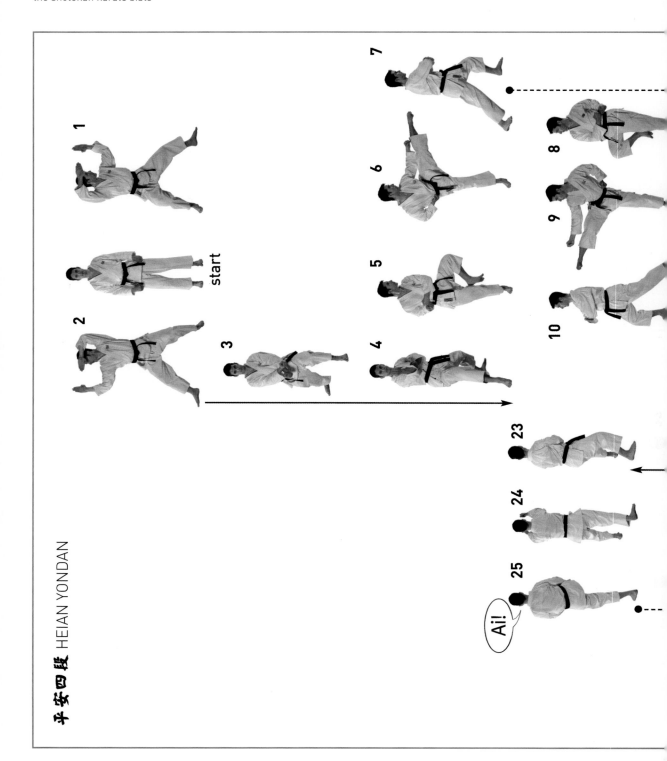

平安四段 HEIAN YONDAN

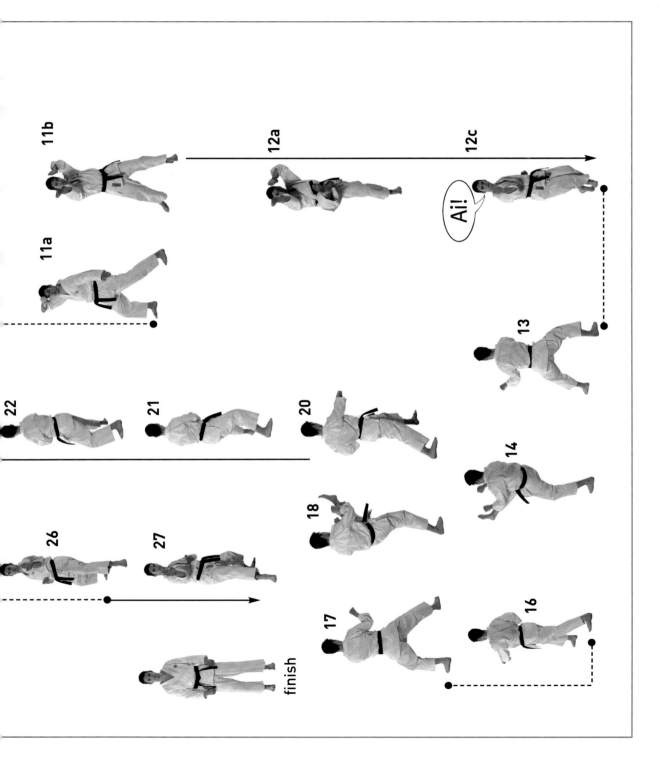

平安五段 HEIAN GODAN

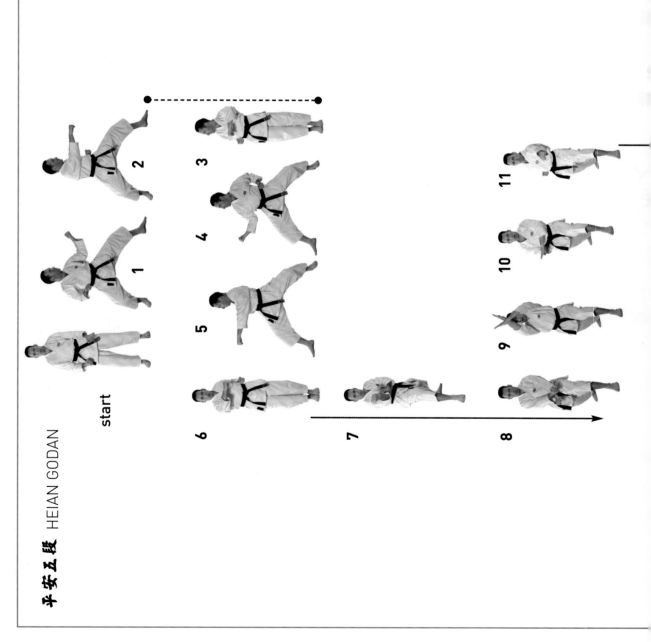

start

1

2

3

4

5

6

7

8

9

10

11

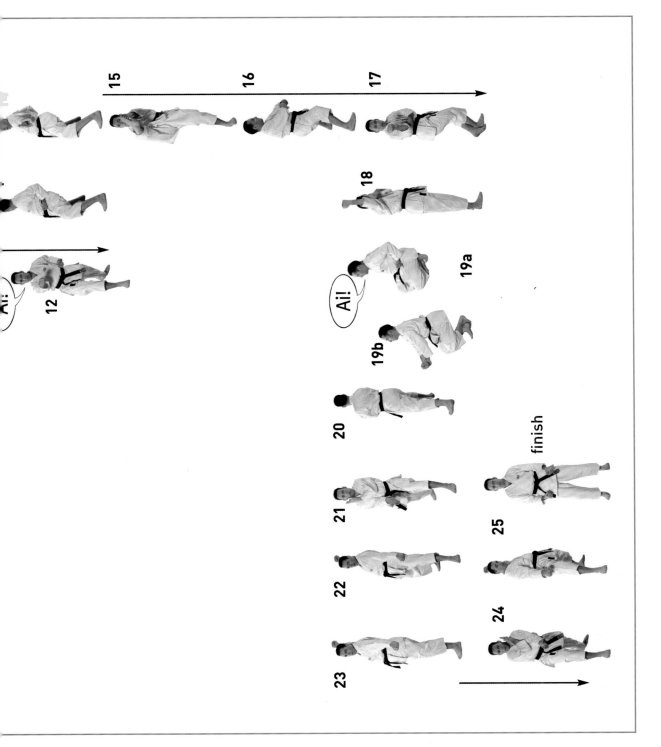

鉄騎初段 TEKKI SHODAN

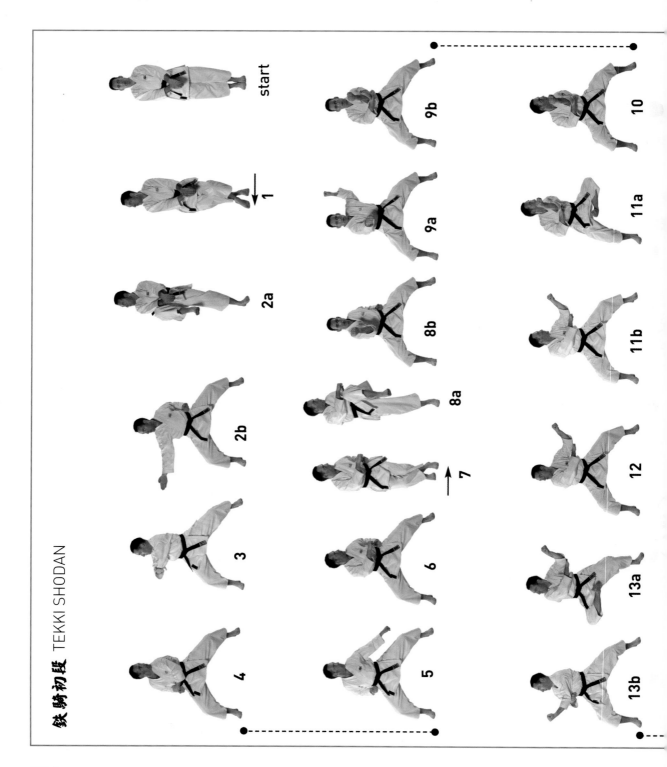

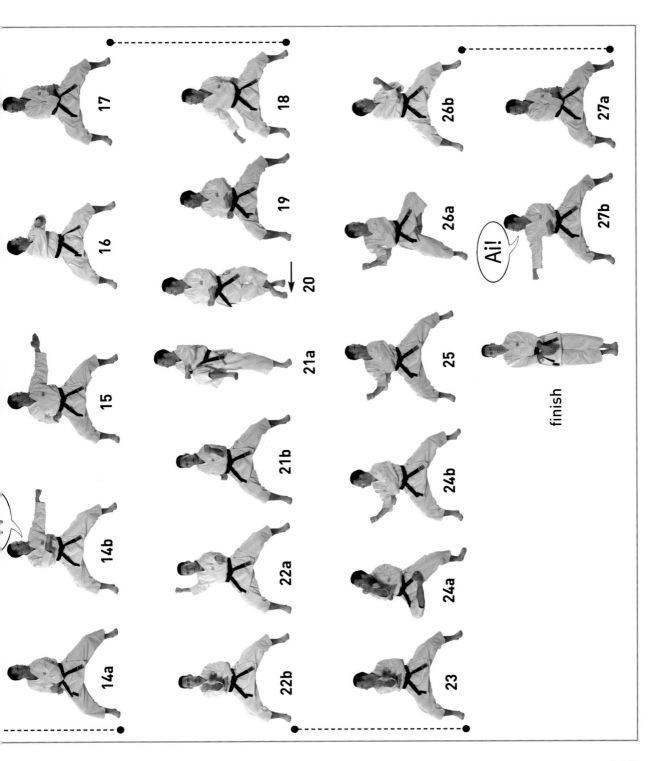

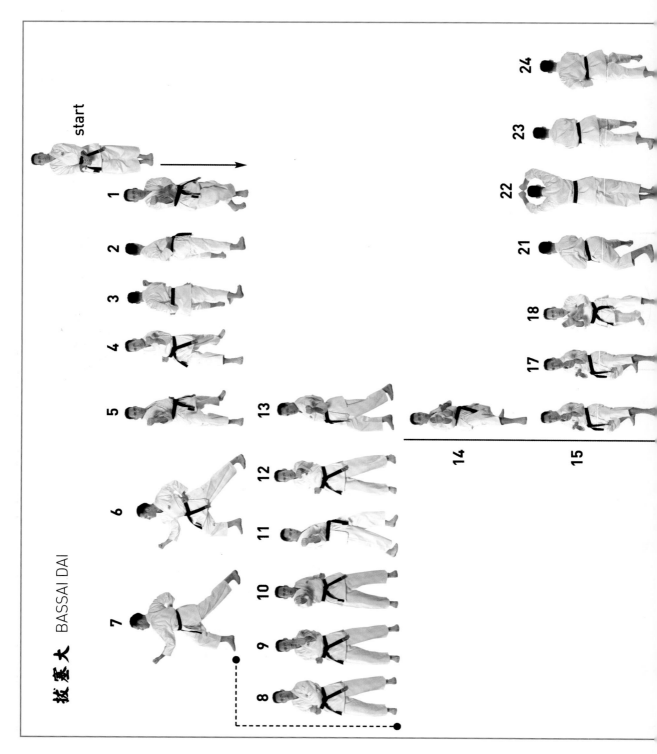

BASSAI DAI

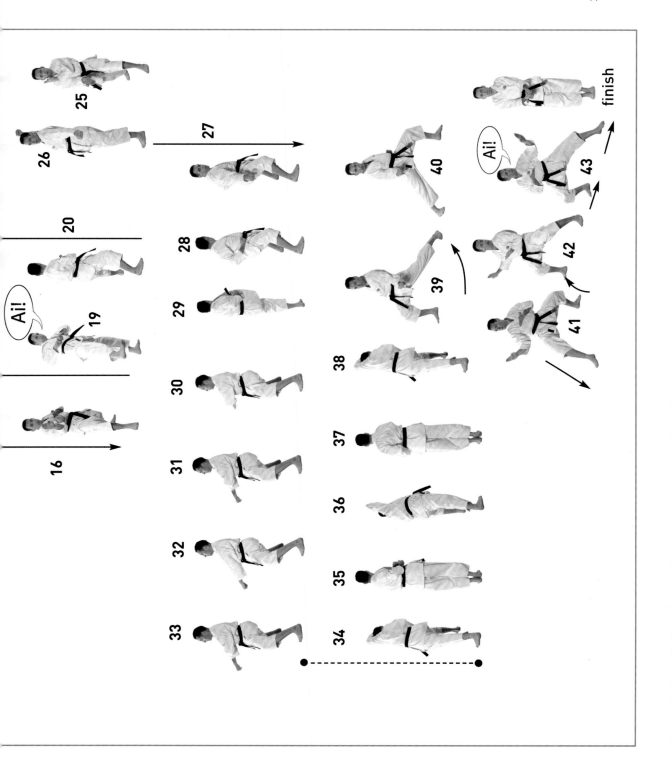

BIBLIOGRAPHY

Abernethy, I. *Bunkai Jutsu*. Neth Publishing, 2002.

Clayton, B. D. *Shotokan's Secret*. Ohara Publications, Inc., 2004.

Egami, S. *The Heart of Karate-do*. Kodansha, 2000.

Funakoshi, G. *Karate Do Kyohan*. Kodansha, 1973.

Funakoshi, G. *Karate Do, My Way of Life*. Kodansha, 1975.

Funakoshi, G. *Karate Do Nyumon*. Kodansha, 1988.

Haines, B. A. *Karate's History and Traditions*. Tuttle, 1995.

Nakayama, M. *Best Karate Volume 5*. Kodansha, 1979.

Nakayama, M. *Best Karate Volume 6*. Kodansha, 1979.

Nakayama, M. *Dynamic Karate*. Kodansha, 1987.

GLOSSARY

Age-uke	Rising block	**Jiyu ippon kumite**	Free one-step sparring
Bassai Dai	Brown belt kata translated as "escape from a castle, primary version" (literally translated as "fortress extraction, large")	**Jiyu kumite**	Free sparring
		Jodan	Head level
		Juji-uke	Cross block
		Kagi-zuki	Hook punch
Budo	Way of the warrior	**Kanji**	Type of ideogram used in the Japanese writing system, literally translated as "Han characters" in reference to the Chinese Han dynasty
Chudan	Stomach level		
Ch'uan fa	Chinese boxing (literally translated as "fist way")		
Dachi	Stance		
Dogi	Karate uniform		
Dojo	Karate training hall, literally translated as "place of the way"	**Kata**	"Form" or "pattern." In the context of karate, this means a sequence of prearranged techniques against imaginary opponents.
Dojo kun	School code, recited in many karate schools at the beginning or end of class		
		Keimochi	Member of the Okinawan nobility
Empi-uchi	Elbow strike. Empi can also be written "enpi," but it is always pronounced "empi."	**Keri**	Kick. When it follows another word, the sound changes to geri, as in mae-geri, mawashi-geri, and so on.
Gedan barai	Downward block (literally translated as "lower-level sweep")	**Kiai**	A martial shout (literally translated as "spirit unity")
Gi	Karate uniform. Short version of dogi.	**Kiba-dachi**	Horse-riding stance
		Kihon	Basic
Gohon kumite	Five-step sparring	**Kime**	Literally translated as "decision." To focus all your energy into a technique.
Gyaku-zuki	Reverse punch		
Hajime	Begin		
Heian	Peace. Shotokan karate contains five Heian kata: Heian Shodan, Heian Nidan, Heian Sandan, Heian Yondan, and Heian Godan.	**Kizami-zuki**	Jabbing punch
		Kokutsu-dachi	Back stance
		Kosa-dachi	Crossed leg stance
		Kumite	Sparring
Heiko-dachi	Parallel-feet stance	**Mae-geri**	Front kick
Heisoku-dachi	Formal attention stance (literally translated as "closed feet stance")	**Manji-uke**	Swastika block
		Mawashi-geri	Roundhouse kick
Ippon kumite	One-step sparring	**Mawatte**	Turn

Mikazuki-geri	Crescent kick		**Tate shuto-uke**	Vertical knife-hand block
Mokuso	Meditate		**Tekki**	Iron Horse. Shotokan karate contains three Tekki kata: Tekki Shodan, Tekki Nidan, and Tekki Sandan.
Morote-uke	Double-handed block			
Musubi-dachi	Informal attention stance (literally translated as "connected stance")			
Nagashi-uke	Passing block		**Tetsui-uchi**	Hammer fist strike
Naha-te	Okinawan unarmed fighting style, from the port town of Naha		**Tode**	Okinawan unarmed fighting style, literally translated as "Chinese fist"
Nami gaeshi-geri	Returning wave kick		**Tsukami-uke**	Grasping block
Naore	Relax (literally translated as "put back into place")		**Tsuki**	Punch (literally translated as "thrust"). The Tsu sound changes whenever it follows another word, so tsuki becomes zuki in oi-zuki, gyaku-zuki, and so on.
Nukite-uchi	Spear-hand strike			
Oi-zuki	Stepping punch (literally translated as a "chasing punch")			
Osae-uke	Pressing block		**Uchi-uke**	Inside block
Pinan	Original Okinawan name for Heian, meaning "peace"		**Ude-uke**	Forearm block
			Uke	Usually interpreted as a block in karate but literally translated, it means "reception." Judo and jujitsu practitioners call the person who is thrown the uke the receiver. Karate practitioners might refer to the defender as the ukete, the receiving hand.
Randori	Literally translated as "disordered engagement"			
Rei	Bow			
Samurai	Japanese feudal warrior			
Sanbon kumite	Three-step sparring			
Seiretsu	Line up			
Sensei	Teacher			
Shiai kumite	Tournament sparring		**Uraken-uchi**	Backfist strike
Shizen-tai	Literally translated as "natural body"		**Ushiro-geri**	Back kick
			Yama-zuki	Mountain punch
Shodan	First level. A 1st degree black belt is called a shodan.		**Yame**	Stop
			Yasume	Rest
Shuri	Historic capital of Okinawa, influential in the creation of karate		**Yoi**	Ready
			Yoi-dachi	Ready stance
Shuri-te	Okinawan unarmed fighting style, from the royal city of Shuri		**Yoko keage**	Side rising kick
			Yoko kekomi	Side thrusting kick
Shuto-uchi	Knife-hand strike		**Yori ashi**	Sliding foot movement where the front foot moves first
Shuto-uke	Knife-hand block			
Soto-uke	Outside block		**Zenkutsu-dachi**	Front stance

INDEX